TESTIMONIALS

"Beyond Ally is definitely a step in the direction towards the true liberation of people of color and the progress of all people. Ownership of dismantling systemic oppression belongs to us all, white people not being exempt. If ever there was a hand-book to lead the way, this is it. It is truly inspiring, something that we all need to read, and all need to work!"

Aida Rodriguez
Comedian, Actress, Writer, and Activist

"This is a critical moment in our country's history, and defeating systemic inequality will take allies who are committed to learning what it really means to fight racial injustice. An important and timely book, 'Beyond Ally' offers a detailed road map for those of us who want to help build a more just and equitable world."

Peter T. Grauer
Chairman of the Board, Bloomberg LP

"At this moment in time, a swell of white people are recognizing their role in the racism that pervades our planet. The risk to this movement is helpless paralysis when the full scope of the problem is realized. Dr. Akbar warmly invites the reader into the challenging process of self-reflection and encourages them to engage in the work of racial justice. Beyond Ally is an expertly timed road map for white people ready to address how race and racism impact their lives."

Candice Norcott, PhD
University of Chicago
Department of Psychiatry and Behavioral Neuroscience

"As the world may now be ready to tackle systemic racism, Dr. Akbar highlights the important role white people can play as agents of change and allies for racial justice. *Beyond Ally* positions, in a real and actionable way, a concept of everyday allyship which is intentional and consistent in order to support people who truly seek to commit to taking a stand against racism and make a difference."

Erika Irish Brown
Chief Diversity Officer
Goldman Sachs

"Dr. Akbar tells it like it is and tells it like it should be told. She writes a raw and honest book about race, whiteness, the racial trauma that lives in our communities and in our bodies. She gives readers, especially white readers, a blueprint for how to begin the process of moving beyond allyship into becoming more active agents of change."

Dena Simmons, Ed.D
Assistant Director at Yale Center for Emotional Intelligence

"As a Hmong American woman psychologist, the personal stories of racism that the author shared resonated with so many of my own. To me, this confirms the need to move beyond being an ally. This book has the potential to start powerful conversations and personal growth. The author presents thought-provoking questions- yet the work toward change remains in the hands of the reader and the author is very clear about that. This is a much-needed book!"

Talee Vang, PsyD., LP
Expert in diversity, equity, trauma, and health psychology

"I am a White woman who grew up in racially segregated Louisville, Kentucky. Because my working-class family was fairly open to other cultures, and because I had the opportunity to live and work with Indigenous communities in Latin America, I thought I had no prejudices. Was I ever wrong! Reading Dr. Akbar's book woke me up to the multitude of ways that "kindhearted" people like me are oblivious of the deep racism in our core. Thank you for educating us, Dr. Akbar."

—Millie Grenough
Author of Oasis in the Overwhelm, Clinical Instructor in Psychiatry, Yale University School of Medicine

"At once intensely personal and analytical, Beyond Ally is a major contribution to our understanding of the ways in which each of us can confront systemic racism that has afflicted our nation from the beginning. The book offers a comprehensive roadmap that will enable White people to better understand their privilege and embrace anti-racist attitudes and behavior. The pursuit of racial justice requires building transformative alliances and Dr. Maysa Akbar is an effective and insightful guide on this long-overdue journey."

—Steve Grossman, CEO
Initiative for a Competitive Inner City

BEYOND
ALLY

BEYOND ALLY

THE PURSUIT OF RACIAL JUSTICE

SUPPORTER | ALLY | ADVOCATE | ACCOMPLICE | EQUITY BROKER

DR. MAYSA AKBAR

PUBLISH YOUR PURPOSE PRESS

Publish Your Purpose Press
141 Weston Street, #155
Hartford, CT, 06141

The opinions expressed by the Author are not necessarily those held by Publish Your Purpose Press.

Ordering Information: Quantity sales and special discounts are available on quantity purchases by corporations, associations, and others. For details, contact the publisher at orders@publishyourpurposepress.com.

Edited by: Malka Wickramatilake
Cover design by: Ryan Lause
Typeset by: Medlar Publishing Solutions Pvt Ltd., India
Stock photos provided by Unsplash

Printed in the United States of America.
ISBN: 978-1-951591-40-3 (hardcover)
ISBN: 978-1-951591-38-0 (paperback)
ISBN: 978-1-951591-39-7 (ebook)

Library of Congress Control Number: 2020911173

First edition, July 2020

Publish Your Purpose Press works with authors, and aspiring authors, who have a story to tell and a brand to build. Do you have a book idea you would like us to consider publishing? Please visit PublishYourPurposePress.com for more information.

EPIGRAPH

For the gift of MELANIN.

For the generations of relentless women in my family, past, present, and future:

my grandmother, Albertina, captive,
sold into indentured servitude.
PEACEKEEPER.

my mother, Olga, victim, third grade
education, immigrant.
FACTORY WORKER.

me, Maysa, survivor, first generation
college student, homeowner.
CYCLE BREAKER.

my daughter, Kalilah, thriving
academic genius, athlete.
OPPORTUNITY CREATOR.

CONTENTS

PART III: THE PURSUIT OF RACIAL JUSTICE

FOREWORD

by Justin Tranter

Justin is a songwriter, singer, and activist. He is also a board member of the Gay & Lesbian Alliance Against Defamation (GLAAD), an organization that promotes LGBTQIA+ acceptance in the entertainment and news industries. His advocacy also includes bringing about the release of the charity single "Hands" to raise funds for Equality Florida Pulse Victims Fund.

Justin was honored with the 2019 ACLU of Southern California's Bill of Rights Award for activism and being an outspoken and powerful voice for the LGBTQIA+ community, diversity, the climate crisis, arts education, animal rights, and ending gun violence. Justin is also a longtime vegan and a supporter of Mercy for Animals.

As someone who has self-identified as an ally to people of color for years, this book has blown my mind. Not because it was a few hours of me shouting at the pages "See, this is what I've been trying to tell y'all for years," but because it showed me where I could do better, where I could grow, and where I was straight up wrong.

See, I've already gotten it wrong in my first sentence! I have NO business self-identifying as an ally. Just because I was lucky enough to go to a racially diverse arts high school, and because I still talk to the best friends I made there, Thomasina and Coco, every single day since the '90s, does not automatically qualify me as an ally. Just because I have signed many people of color (POCs) to my recording and publishing companies, it does not automatically make me an ally. Just because I'm a femme queer who is also "othered," I am not automatically an ally. This is a title earned by putting in the work, each and every day; work on myself, work on the industry I'm part of, and work on all the White people around me.

As I read Dr. Akbar's powerful words, I remember a time in high school where a suburban White train conductor questioned the authenticity of my Black friend's train ticket over and over. After the conductor walked away, I of course sympathized with my friend about how unfair it was. But while he was interrogating my friend, I was too fragile, or maybe too comfortable, to use my White privilege to defend my friend who felt so powerless and so embarrassed. A true ally would have said something.

I CAN do better.

While reading *Beyond Ally*, I recall a few years ago when I was asked to be a co-host for a LGBTQ music business brunch. When they told me names of the other co-hosts, who were all White cis men, I immediately responded with, "I won't be a co-host unless the other hosts are more diverse in terms of race and gender." I was very proud of my allyship and gave myself a big social justice pat on the back. Their response was "OK, well then you don't have to be a co-host, but please still come, we promise you the guest list is diverse." As I walked in, my heart sank because there was only one woman there and not one POC. A true ally would have never shown up and supported an event they knew wasn't interested in being diverse and inclusive.

I CAN do better.

Just a few days ago, Shea Diamond, a Black trans singer signed to my company, called me to talk about a microaggression she was facing. Before I did the right thing and told her I would make some calls on her behalf to address it, I first did the wrong thing and said, "You're going to have to grow a thicker skin if you want to survive this business." A true ally would do everything in their power to create a better world, and never put any responsibility on the person experiencing the hardship and prejudice.

I CAN do better.

I WANT to do better.

This book has lit a fire in me; my eyes are open. I'm fully aware that I need to show up, be about it, and do MORE. *Beyond Ally* has motivated me to walk the walk, not just talk the talk. I will take the steps necessary to create systemic change in my professional life. I commit to working with POCs in my career to create an affirming, supportive place for colleagues experiencing microaggressions. In my personal life, I commit to spreading information and awareness about allyship. I commit to learning more about the power of the LGBTQIA+ as allies in racial justice. This is my personal call to action, my renewed commitment.

I WILL DO BETTER.

This book is a tool. This book is a cure. But you have to be willing to open your polluted little White heart and put these tools to work to cure it. If you are very new to your ally journey, or someone like me who thought you had it figured out for decades, I promise you there is more work to do. Thankfully, Dr. Akbar has given us the steps, but we, White people, have to actually take them.

The time to do better is NOW.

ACKNOWLEDGMENTS

Writing a second book, another powerful piece that I dream will positively impact our world, was a labor of love for me and a deep expression of my life's dedication to racial justice. Many of us who are trying to change the world in one way or another are individually recognized and praised for the work that we do. In reality, we could never get it all done without our team of soldiers who often go unrecognized. For me, they live gracefully behind the scenes, empowering me, building me up, protecting me, running logistics for me, managing my schedule, making sure I eat and stay healthy, and ensuring that the coffee supply never runs low.

None of this would have been possible without my dedicated team. To everyone at Integrated Wellness Group, the amazing company I am honored to serve as Founder and CEO, thank you for showing up every day and helping uplift people of color throughout the two pandemics we have faced this year. Many of you have stood by my side for almost a decade and deserve to be acknowledged publicly as extraordinary human beings. To the best allies I have ever had the pleasure of working with and sharing part of my life's journey: Jessica Mommens, you are my right-hand woman, my rock, and my anchor. You are the yin to my yang, and I could not have picked a better person as my work wife. Lisa Votto, I stand in so much gratitude for your consistent, grounding words; counsel; hours of editing; and input into this book. Your feedback was beyond valuable, and the book is stronger than ever because of your input. Emmanuel Silva De Sousa, you are a gem, one of the smartest people I know. I thank you for believing in this work and for dedicating yourself to making sure all my dreams come true. The world is a better place because you are in it. Osieca Samuel, thank you for keeping me sane, laughing at my corny jokes, keeping my schedule tight, and creating a steel wall around me so that I can be creative and innovative.

To the IWG team and clinicians, thank you for relentlessly serving our community that is hurting, many from racial trauma, and supporting them through the toughest time in their lives.

To my business mentor, Carlton Highsmith, who never saw my age, my race, or my shortfalls. Carlton, you just saw someone who was hungry to learn, hungry to grow, and hungry to succeed. You have never stopped me, thrown away any of my wild ideas; you have only encouraged and supported me.

Writing a book about how to be more than just an ally for people of color across the globe was demanding, especially given the context of what was happening around the world. There are a number of people who supported me and carried me through the writing process. I want to lift Mariyah Charlton for being rock-solid in this entire process. Maryiah, you did not hesitate to support me in the research and literature review, making sure that this project kept going; although I wanted to give it up many times, you have stood by me during every struggle and all my successes. A very special thanks to my publisher, Jenn Grace, for pushing me to write this book, and my project manager, Bailly Morse. I'm forever indebted to Malka Wickramatilake, Gail Marlene Schartz, and Wendy Jo Dymond for their editorial help, keen insight, and ongoing encouragement in bringing my stories to life. It is because of them that I was able to complete this book in four weeks rather than the six- to eight-month timeframe that was originally set as the release date. You all knew that this book would provide a much-needed guide for the groundbreaking work on allyship. We did it!

To my loving and caring family. To Rahsaan, for always being the person I could turn to, my confidant, my best friend, my partner, and, most of all, the love of my life. To my beautiful little family who sustained me in ways that I never knew I needed. To Kalilah, for making sure that all of the technical aspects of this book, including the title, were on point and for having endless debates with me about race and the role of allyship. You are and continue to be our ancestors' wildest dream, and I love you to pieces. To Kyoshi, my rock and my biggest supporter, thank you for making me become the mother I never dreamed I could be.

I'm eternally grateful to my family and close friends, many of whom have taught me discipline, tough love, tenacity, grit, and so much more that has helped me succeed in life. I truly have no idea where I'd be if I did not have a village behind me. To the extended family, DeJesus, Zuniga, Garabot, Akbar, and the Richards-Gulson clan: I learn every day from each of you. To my best sister-friend in the entire world, Dr. Michell Tollinchi: Michell, you are truly the sister I never had, but always wanted. To Kim and Theron Grant, not sure if life would be complete without your sense of humor, laughter, and love. To Carol, Jose, Adriana, and Alyssa Ruiz, my sanity depends on our family time together; you bring me pure joy. To LaNae N. Shelton, your steadfast, guiding presence in my life nurtures my soul. Finally, to all those who have been a part of my accomplishments: my sorors of Delta Sigma Theta Sorority, Inc., the mothers of Jack and Jill of America, Inc., friends, followers, and supporters, thank you for giving me life and motivating me to extend myself beyond my comfort zone. For all of you, for our communities, and for generations to come, I promise to keep fighting.

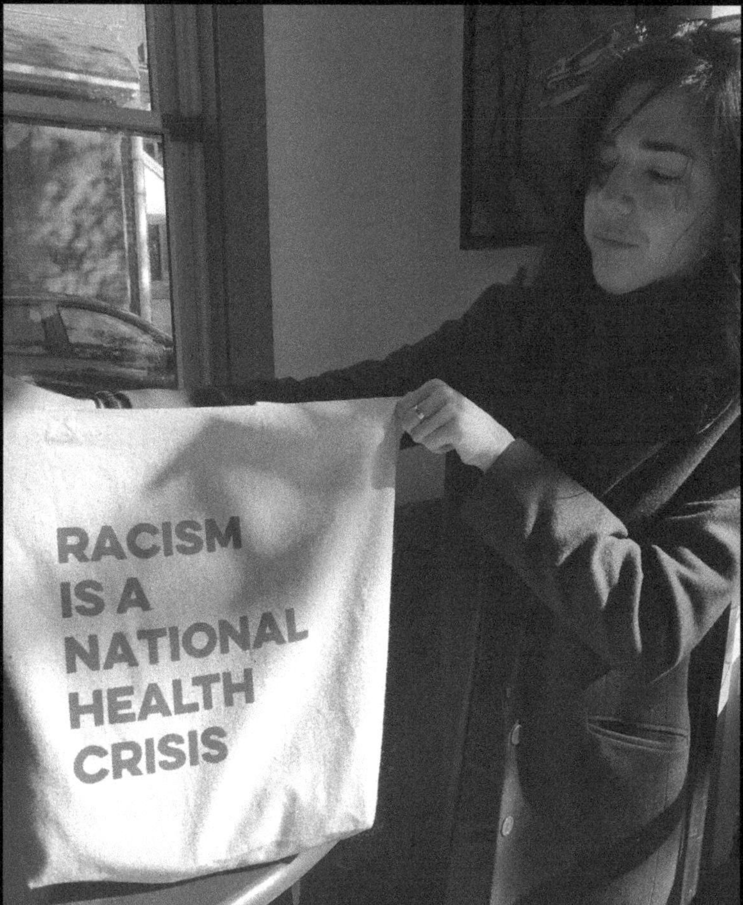
RACISM
IS A
NATIONAL
HEALTH
CRISIS

PREFACE

Welcome. You are here to learn about being an effective ally. You may have many reasons why you picked up this book. Maybe you've been moved by the suffering of people of color at the hands of police. Maybe you've seen the impact of racism on friends of color and want to do more. Maybe you want to more fully live your values of equity and justice.

Engaging in allyship work can be profoundly transformational to you as an individual. It can help you develop skills such as being honest and direct in a conflict, listening deeply to others who are different from you, and sharing leadership. It can help you start stripping off layers of the colonizer mentality and bring you into a more peaceful and loving relationship with the world around you. It can help you accept and even love the parts of yourself you've been taught need to be shamed or hidden. It can help you let go of the pursuit of materialism and welcome in love, friendship, celebration, connection, and authenticity. It can deepen your spirituality or bring in a different spiritual dimension to your life.

To achieve allyship, we will have to talk about some difficult things. I ask that you stay committed to the process. When we are healing from things that cause us or others harm, the initial part of the journey is very hard. It takes a lot of courage to decide to be someone different from what you have been taught. I am invested in guiding you through this work because most often change happens when we are feeling uncomfortable.

We are at a global tipping point but to be successful, the movement needs White people to tackle racism. A colleague, Mercy Quaye, founder of the Narrative Project, always says, "Racism is not a problem created by people of color, it is a White person's problem, so White people must take ownership in fixing it." Unfortunately, some White people are still trapped by traditions of being beneficiaries of systemic racism. Imagine if each White citizen who reads this book decided to dedicate themselves to racial justice work. A completely different quality of life would be possible to achieve. The difficulty in shedding the layers is more than worthwhile. When you ally the right way, you can literally help change the world. But the key word here is *right*. For allies to be successful, all efforts are to be grounded in anti-racism, accountability, and creating space for people of color.

INTRODUCTION

WHITE PEOPLE. DO SOMETHING.

A few years ago I was invited to a town hall-style TV segment at BRIC TV in Brooklyn, where the topic was mental health as a civil right for people of color (POCs), perhaps the only type of reparation Black and Brown people will ever receive for the years of inhumane torture and brutality experienced at the hands of colonizers and slave owners. The conversation around reparation was deep, raw, and dynamic, given the different opportunities we have in this country to repair the harm that has been done and truly restore humanity.

After the segment, two White millennials introduced themselves to me as racial justice activists. These individuals were struck by the panel of passionate POCs and freedom fighters who addressed racial injustice during the live taping. They approached me with intention and asked a very specific question:

> Dr. Akbar, we are White, we work with children of color in Brooklyn, we want to be allies, but we do not know what we are doing. We know that we have bias and that generations of our family were probably complicit in what has happened to Black people and immigrants in this country. Do you have any suggestions, recommendations, or a road map? We know it is not right for us to define what a good ally looks like; after all, we as White people have historically and continue, even in the area of diversity and inclusion, to claim territory and take it over. We have no idea what it feels like to be Black or Brown in a "post-racial" America. Please help.

I often have to think on my feet, knowing that this may be the only opportunity I will have to plant a seed. Such was the case in this situation. For these two young racial justice warriors, who "happen to be" White, to correctly enter into their journey as allies, I knew this moment was critical.

My answer to them is this book.

The topic of anti-racism and racial justice is a sensitive one for most White people. It's a conversation that many avoid because often beliefs, values, and emotions around race tend to run high. The United States has had a long history of generational struggle around how we define humanity and who exactly is accepted in that elite club. Globally, the world faces similar issues. Many countries have begun acknowledging their roles in the dark history of racism and oppression, trying to find a new path closer to a reckoning, to reconciliation, and to harmony. For instance, countries have paid reparations to people they have harmed. Examples include the United Kingdom, which paid 19.9£ (25 million US dollars) to Kenyans (Nymark 2015); Germany, which paid $89 billion to Holocaust survivors over the course of 6 decades (Eddy 2012); and South Africa, paid $85 million to victims of apartheid (Matthew 2014). Even the US paid $1.6 billion to Japanese Americans for World War II (Howard-Hassman 2019).

But unfortunately, despite the struggle, the United States has not acknowledged or made amends for the emotional, psychological, physical, and financial harm against the Indigenous and Black communities. This is, in part, because here in America, racism is conceptualized through the lenses of denial and capitalism. The script for White people is "I am not to blame for the sins of my ancestors, stop crying over something that happened so long ago, grab yourself by the bootstraps and just get over it!" Unfortunately, the choice to tackle historical racism in this way has not worked. So, as a result, tension continues to build; the country becomes more polarized; people are hurting, even dying; and traumatic experiences are normalized.

There are endless daily news stories highlighting death at the hands of brutal police violence: National Football League players taking a knee against the principles of the national anthem to protest how "liberty and justice for all" does not apply to Black people in America. Border patrol abuse. Dehumanizing conditions in detention centers where Latinx immigrants are held. Religious targeting of Muslims due to ignorance, fear, and propaganda. The appropriateness of dreadlocks or natural hair in the workplace, schools, or during sports competitions. If you are not White, every aspect of your life is up for debate and highly controversial, often centered on its suitability compared to White norms and anchored in White privilege. Racism—and by extension trauma—is as old as creation.

This book is not intended to reveal what we don't already know; it is intended to provide a guide for those wanting to use their privilege in service of anti-racism and to do something about their entitlement to create an America that honors justice for all. This book is geared toward connecting dots that were separately categorized in our minds but now require inclusion. We cannot change what we do not know and what we do not own. This book represents that journey: acknowledgment, owning, choosing to change. Review, recycle, and repeat.

Allyship begins by reconciling with the history of racism and truly achieving racial justice. White people have a responsibility to own their role in creating, sustaining, and elevating Whiteness for their financial, social, and political gain. The way this works is by accepting the sins of their White ancestors, dealing with the White guilt that follows, and leading the change within the White community in an effort to dismantle structural and institutionalized racism. Side note: Notice I said leading the change in White communities, not Black, Latinx, Indigenous, and/or any other oppressed racial groups. White people need to deal with White people.

This type of dramatic change requires a shift in the moral compass and definition of Whiteness whereby dealing with White fragility is a logical, yet crucial, next step. What this means is generating the essential fortitude to deal with the consequences of one's actions and the legacy of one's family. This legacy shows up in the simplest attribute, which is the twin lies of White superiority and Black inferiority, two interconnected myths that the Community Healing Network (CHN) has made its mission to dispel. If one went as far back as possible, how was generational wealth obtained by your family? Was it through enslavement, racism, and oppression? Maybe there is no generational wealth stemming from these things, but if there is, it is the responsibility of White people to uncover their past and reckon with the truths that are found. Once White people are able to own their role, then and only then can we have a substantial conversation about how we will end racism: one person, one neighborhood, one community at a time. Although this process will not undo the harm that has been caused, it will create a safe starting place to move toward reconciliation, repairing relationships, and healing.

Before we get into the material, I want to share a short yet poignant statement by a Black male who works in a corporate environment. "Not all White people are my enemy. If a White person is standing in the way of my progress, then yes, he is my enemy." This statement is so powerful. I similarly believe that not all White people are bad, not all White people are our enemies, not all White people are White supremacists or believe in a racial hierarchy. Of course, there are some who do, but they are probably not reading this book!

That said, I also want to warn against the desire to take charge and dictate to POCs what they need to diminish problems in their communities. Deciding to become an ally, informed by a POC who is best suited to take the helm in matters of allyship, is truly the first step of this process. For that reason, I encourage you to enter into this journey with humility, an open mind, and a loving heart. You are going to read things that will be tough to digest. It is never easy to face the reflection in the mirror of past generations, and ask, "Who am I? Where did I truly come from? And who do I want to be/become?" Open your mind, question your beliefs and where they came from. Listen and participate in tough conversations, with yourself and with POCs, while reading this book. I have confidence that you will be successful in your journey toward allyship and beyond.

I emphasized to the two budding allies from the BRIC TV audience that combating racism and becoming a true champion for racial justice can be difficult for those who are unsure of what to say, how to act, or how to show up. It is OK to be a student and to learn the right way. Take your time, check in with people who are conscientious, and get real feedback on how you are doing with your process. White allyship is a journey that if you choose to take on, you will be able to change yourself, socialize your children to be tolerant and inclusive, and influence your family and community to embrace equity and harmony.

Here are five simple steps I provided the two millennials, to start working on their allyship process right now:

1. Acknowledge the true role of racism, at minimum, from the time of enslavement until now. It is not something that happened to Black people, it is something that was done to Black people by your people.
2. There is power in acknowledging your guilt. It is the most freeing experience. It is the ultimate motivator to enact change, it can give individuals an opportunity to repair the harm done, it allows for making amends, and it challenges the current structurally racist systems that are kept alive for White supremacy. Also, it is the truest form of restorative justice.

3. Do not assume to know the struggle of POCs or have answers to our problems.

4. Do not give yourself any title, such as ally, that you have not earned.

5. If you want to do this social/racial justice thing right, remain humble, respectful, and eager to learn. Do not engage in victimhood and, under no circumstances see yourself, in words or deed, as a savior.

EQUAL RIGHTS
FOR OTHERS
DOES NOT MEAN
FEWER RIGHTS
FOR YOU.
THIS ISN'T A PIE.

CHAPTER 1

HISTORY OF TRAUMA

In the book *My Grandmother's Hands: Racialized Trauma and the Pathway to Mending Our Hearts and Bodies*, Resmaa Menakem (2017) eloquently illustrates that long before White people began hurting Black people, they were brutalizing one another, dating back to the 1500s. Citizens were burned at the stake, a tradition that continued on into the transatlantic slave trade. Europeans often beat, kidnapped, chained, and tortured one another, sometimes even pulling human bodies apart, a sadistic technique used as an official instrument of punishment. In fact, during the Middle Ages, violence was a form of entertainment. Menakem remarks that it is no wonder tortured Europeans fled to America because they were either traumatized by the savagery or by watching vulgar brutality.

In the 16th century, when the English arrived in North America, Menakem (2017, 81) states that "they brought much of their resilience, much of their brutality and, I believe, a great deal of their trauma with them." This was clearly observed in the similarity of their cruelty toward slaves. Like in their native countries, Europeans in the New World adapted the long-standing and violent White-on-White practices.

Menakem (2017) goes on to state that in the 16th century, the concept of Whiteness and race was invented to establish "White-body supremacy." Europeans unable to process their own trauma displaced it on Black and Native bodies to justify the colonization, abuse, and enslavement of people of color (POCs). Race is a concept created for the sole advantage of White people to gain dominance over darker peoples instead of causing friction between one another. For this reason, many White people have little regard for Black people and often forget that they are human. As tradition holds, White people desired to colonize the mind of POCs and formalize a culture of White superiority, creating a sense of hatred for Black people.

Generation after generation of Black bodies have stored up White trauma, now coined race-based trauma, which originated from intense survival energy. Menakem (2017, 88) emphasizes that "[r]ace is a myth, but a myth with teeth and claws. Institutions, structures, beliefs, and narratives have been centered around it. Until we recognize it for the collective delusion it is, it might as well be real."

As an ally, it is important to do the personal work around the cycle of violence. It is important to recognize the power structures in your own family and make a connection as to how anger is projected to the powerless in society. Researchers of violence have noted that it is the internalization of hatred that often leads people to project their hatred and violence onto others. This same theory holds true in interactions between White people and other races. White racism is anchored in power and control, just like the cycle of violence in families. The batterer, and often the victim, are in denial, and there are three phases: tension building, acute explosion, and honeymoon. Fear will, most often, cause those in the White dominant culture to project their irrational perceptions onto POCs (Wilson 2011). To carry on racist ideology White people, just like batterers, have to convince themselves that POCs are less than and not worthy. In actuality, it is the hatred of themselves and their own insecurities that fuel racism.

My professional experience leads me to conclude that White people's fear and trauma are the root of racism. Racism has been such a huge issue in America over the years that some psychiatrists have advocated for making racism a psychiatric disorder. However, the American Psychiatric Association (APA) said that a "social issue" should not be medicalized (Thomas 2014). Although racism is learned behavior, it still demonstrates a projection of delusional and unwarranted hatred toward POC (Bell 2004). Although the APA has never recognized extreme racism as a psychotic disorder, the issue was raised more than 30 years ago by a group of Black psychiatrists

(Poussaint 2002). After several racist killings during the civil rights era, these doctors believed that bigotry had to come from some form of psychosis. However, the step toward a mental health diagnosis was denied due to racism being normalized as a cultural issue rather than psychological (Bell 2004).

Research following World War II demonstrated that anxiety and impulsivity were associated with social bias (Sullaway and Dunbar 1996). The push is for the recognition that anyone who acts harshly or wants to eliminate a group of people based on the color of their skin meets the criteria for a delusional disorder. This would ultimately mean that White people struggling with racism are actually battling a mental illness. Treating racism as normal and not pathological further aids in this disease going untreated. Racism inflicts psychological and physiological pain on people, communities, societies, and the world. It centers on irrational belief systems about a social group and impulsive actions, sometimes leading to mass killings, murder, torture, and death as a result of those belief systems (Rollock and Gordon 2000). Whether recognized as a clinical disorder or not, racism erodes and damages the mental health status of people struggling with it, namely, White people. Seeing racism as a mental illness could further prevent tragic outcomes geared toward POCs.

In many ways, writing about racism and what it has done to White people and racial trauma and what it has done to POCs is personal for me. I truly believe it was the impetus not just in choosing a career in psychology but also in developing a surgeon-like focus on understanding how the social construct of race has evolved, how White people have been the sole benefactors of its creation, how POCs have suffered under its regime, and ultimately how we dismantle it. I wanted to share when it became apparent to me that racism not only existed but that it also was alive and thriving and how two very different attitudes of two professors impacted my education.

URBAN TRAUMA IS RACISM—SURVIVOR

As an immigrant growing up in Brooklyn in a mixed-race neighborhood, during a time when kids played in the street until dark and everyone else's parent was also your parent, I always felt that there was a strong sense of community. It's ironic to say this about New York, but in many ways, I was sheltered from the harsh race-based realities that lived past the borders of my 'hood. What I experienced daily were kids who looked like me and families that looked like mine: a tossed salad of many different people and cultures who all came together during morning rush hour at the corner bodega. Everyone seemed to fit in. It was not a utopia; New York City in the 1980s was not a joke, but it felt familiar and like family.

Later, as an undergraduate student, I was fascinated with how people of African descent survived centuries of brutalization and still survived. I took every African and Caribbean studies course offered. This burning question became one of the reasons I wanted to examine human behavior and, after obtaining my undergraduate degree, went to Florida A&M University, a historically Black College and University, to study community psychology from the most elite Black psychologists in the country. As a poor, marginalized immigrant woman of color who began to elevate in the educational ladder, I began to experience firsthand the ugliness of racism, and I clearly understood how protected, disillusioned, and naive I was about this country's dark past.

During graduate school at a predominantly White institution (folks of color call these types of schools PWIs), I encountered two types of professors that impacted my life. One was inclusive, open to a diversity of ideas, and supportive. The other was tough, strict, inflexible, and somewhat callous.

The second, a man, demonstrated high expectations from his students, and his demeanor was stern. Although psychology is considered by many as a soft science, this professor was not warm and fuzzy at all. Despite his exterior, I actually found him to be endearing, perhaps because in many ways he reminded me of my father. Although they looked nothing alike, my professor was White, they showed up to the world in the exact same way. For that reason, I was used to the high expectations he held for his students, as well as the feeling of "not good enough" that came along with it. Because I grew up in a very patriarchal family, I normalized this behavior because he was a man, but then the interactions became more and more degrading and insulting over time. I continued justifying his behavior, almost as a survival tactic, and placed the responsibility of those negative and discrediting interactions on myself; this way of coping felt familiar because it is exactly what I did with my dad. It is true that if we do not heal from past pain, patterns simply continue to repeat themselves, skipping from body to body like a disease.

I never considered that he did not like me because of who I was, the color of my skin, and what I represented. Oftentimes, despite the Whitesplaining that happens around this topic, POCs do not initially consider race as the reason for negative interactions with White people—that is, until there is a catalyst event. For me, that moment was a midterm grade I received from this professor in my Theories of Psychotherapy class.

It was the lowest grade in my entire academic career. I was a high-achieving student who consistently carried a high honors/dean list grade point average (GPA) and above in my graduate program, obtaining As in the toughest courses in my field. This class was the cornerstone of psychology. If I was unable to pass this class, it raised the question, why was I there in the first place? How would I be able to accurately do therapy with my patients and create adequate treatment plans? My imposter syndrome was at an all-time high.

I bravely made an appointment to meet with the professor after class. I coached myself the entire morning about how I was going to approach this conversation. I would be humble but motivated. I would want to learn from him and the way he likes students to respond to questions in his exams. I would study what characteristics he liked to see in his students and learn to deliver on those qualities as often as possible. I would ask him if there was anything I could do to bolster my grade in the class, how I could study harder and more efficiently, because only two exams were administered the entire semester. I was ready for this conversation. As a kid growing up in a tough neighborhood, one's emotional intelligence typically falls in the superior range. Studying my professor was as important as the grade.

That afternoon, I walked into his office ready to receive constructive feedback. As a graduate student, you get accustomed to this type of feedback because it happens quite a bit, in nearly all areas of study. Before I was able to say hello and open the conversation with small talk, he asked me to sit down and began to speak:

> Maysa [pronounced incorrectly; he never cared to learn how to say it right, and I stopped trying to correct him], this university is very prestigious. We only accept the best and brightest students. We rank among the top schools in graduate programs of psychology and accept only four students per year. We look for a certain pedigree of students [code for White], and frankly, it is clear to me that you are not from that pedigree. Your performance in my class is substandard, and I just cannot fathom what kind of psychologist you will be if you are unable to pass my psychotherapy class. I seriously think you should reconsider this program, this university, and this field of study. Perhaps you should do something different and open up your slot to a more deserving student.

As the words came out of his mouth, I felt sick to my stomach. I did everything I could to hold back the tears. I was devastated. But most important, he confirmed my worst fear: that I was not good enough. I was, in fact, an imposter, and he had figured me out.

Before I broke down into a pool of hysterical tears, I got up, said nothing, and walked out of his office. I ran into one of the rooms in the clinic and cried for what seemed like hours. I was newly married and called my husband, barely able to speak, trying to get the words out, but only being able to repeat over and over that I was a failure. This moment was critical for me. What my husband said in that instance became a defining moment in my life and taught me a lesson about the kind of person that you need on your team. With love, compassion, and clarity, he asked me to calm down and tell him exactly what happened.

Once he got the gist (my husband is not one that needs every single detail, blow by blow), he said, "Maysa [pronounced correctly], you are strong, you are smart, and you can do this. Let's look at the data. What are your current grades in the program?"

I responded, "All As."

He sighed. "OK, what does that data tell you?" Pause. "Does it confirm what this professor is saying about you?"

Still sobbing in the background, I replied, "No."

"So why would you believe him?"

Another long pause as I processed and calculated and then responded, "Because he is right. I don't have the pedigree. My parents were not doctors, they are not alums of the university, nor do they give thousands of dollars to its endowment. I am a street kid, an immigrant, a nobody. How could I have ever thought that I would become a psychologist? I am just a dreamer. These kinds of achievements do not happen for people like me."

Again, with a thoughtful response, he said, "Who cares what your pedigree is? You need to show them that it doesn't matter what walk of life you are from, as long as you are intelligent, dedicated, and able to compete at the same level as those other White grad students. You can do this! You got this! Now wipe those tears, get up and go back in there, and tell that professor that he is wrong and that you are not going anywhere and you will prove him wrong."

I thanked him for his encouragement, for making me feel empowered during a very devastating moment for me, and for his unconditional love. We hung up. I bravely got up, eyes and face swollen from crying, sniffling as I tried to clear the congestion and regulate my breathing. I stood up, firm, chest wide open, posture straight, and with a conviction of determination that this White man will not tear me down. I thought about every ancestor who was denigrated physically, emotionally, and psychologically. I thought about what they fought for and were subsequently killed for. I allowed my mind to freely enter into a space of calling onto my ancestors for strength and protection as I entered this psychological war zone. I readied myself, putting one foot in front of the other, with those small steps being the only goal.

My feet directed me back into the professor's office. It was an out-of-body experience. He looked up, peering from his reading glasses, as I entered the arch of his doorway. I stood there, paralyzed from the neck down, heavy, heart beating a million miles a minute, he said, "What do you want now? I thought our conversation was over."

I managed to say five words, just five: "**You will not break me!**" Then I left his office, left the building, exited the school parking lot, and cried all the way home.

In full transparency, I spent a few days at home, not going to class, full of shame, and declining toward a very rocky downward spiral. I didn't eat, didn't get out of bed, and spent those few days feeling sorry for myself. I realized at some point that there would only be one outcome: either I win or he wins. The way things were looking, he had the advantage. The joy and passion I felt for psychology had been taken from me.

I was lost after this situation, but there was one professor in the department who noticed. Her allyship was still in development back then as she herself was struggling with being an "other" as a White lesbian woman. I shared with her my situation, and she was able to empathize with what I had gone through. I noticed that she was more inclusive, being one of the only professors who actively sought out students of color to work in her lab. She was also very supportive of thesis and dissertation topics that centered on diverse populations and cross-cultural psychological research, even though that was not her area of specialty. She was very nurturing and caring, and she provided moral support. This professor was aware of the adversities I overcame to become a first-generation graduate student. She encouraged me to use those survival tactics to develop thick skin and push forward. I also noticed she did many low-key things and sometimes took risks to make a difference for students of color. Throughout my graduate program, there were some subtle ways she made a difference, without necessarily positioning herself as a hero.

In spite of good intentions, her allyship was flawed. For example, she was unable, due to her own oppression, to advocate for me and challenge institutional bias and discrimination. Her recommendations often left me alone to cope with the situation, as it placed the responsibility on me, as the person harmed by racism, to solve the problem. As an ally, it would have been much more helpful if she would have challenged the male professor as a colleague, spoken up against this type of behavior in departmental meetings, created a safe space for me to process my grievances, and provided me with clear steps on the policies and procedures for students who encounter discrimination. Even so, her actions absolutely made a positive difference to me.

With the support of my allied professor, I was able to find my grit and determination, and I went back to school and finished my degree, graduating summa cum laude with a 3.906 cumulative GPA. I received a B– in that psychotherapy class, the only B in my entire graduate career. I already knew I had to work twice as hard to compete with my White counterparts in addition to having to prove myself to a racist professor. Later, I was accepted by the Yale School of Medicine, Child Study Center for my pre- and postdoctoral training. Only one other student before me, who ironically was also a POC *and* an immigrant, was selected for this prestigious training program.

Although it was satisfying to have proved him wrong by successfully graduating top of my class and putting our university on the map for trainees gaining acceptance to an Ivy League fellowship, this was an underwhelming win for me. I moved on, and in 2013, I received a call from the university alumni office informing me that I had been selected for their most highly regarded Alumni Award. In fact, it was the first time anyone from the School of Social Sciences had been selected for this award, which was typically reserved for candidates from the School of Medicine or the Law School. I was also the first woman of color to receive this award.

I remember how proud my White ally professor looked when she witnessed me getting this award, and I wondered if she had nominated me. I remember looking out into the audience and seeing her, feeling her allyship, the first I had ever experienced. At that moment; I knew she had done something good not just for me but for other students of color too. As for the psychotherapy professor, he didn't attend the awards ceremony, but it did not matter because I knew my ally professor and I had proved him wrong. I did have the pedigree to be an outstanding psychologist and to make incredible contributions to the field of psychology. My ally professor, me, and this book are just a few of many examples of why true allyship matters so much.

Moments like this one with both of these professors, over 15 years ago now, seem like a blip on the radar of my life. I can remember the situation so well because it was such a deep emotional injury for me. As I retell this story, I am clear in my maturity, of the role that both racism and allyship occupied during those few years until I graduated. This situation so early in my development as a psychologist allowed me to take away meaningful lessons, many of which I hope to share with you in order to bring clarity to a highly complex human flaw and ways for White people to start changing it.

In the last two decades, racial trauma has become the central point of scientific study in my professional career. My research has focused on racial identity and racial socialization to understand the role of resilience in the Black community. My career as a psychologist, much like society, took many twists and turns in my quest to identify the intersectionality between race and trauma. Most of all, the mental health of POCs was a complex puzzle that I needed to piece together. In my first book, *Urban Trauma: A Legacy of Racism* (Akbar 2017), I outline the psychological and biological damage enacted by enslavement and how structural racism from poverty, overcrowded housing, poor physical and mental health, despair, violence, crime, and drug abuse are at the center of our urban communities as a result of historical oppression. These conditions create a type of chronic race-based toxic stress that leads to dysfunctional characteristics and behaviors that lie beneath the surface of many diverse peoples and communities. In combination, these components genetically variate a POC's DNA and thereby how they show up in the world. As my career continues evolving, I am starting to see a semblance of what this puzzle may look like. I keenly understand the importance of healing for POCs through acknowledgment, validation, and recognition for the harm that was done by

White people. Equally important is the work White people must do, both on themselves and in their families and communities. This work will begin to create a new world that dismantles racism one system at a time, together. It is my hope that if you are a White ally reading this book, you have this same conviction in your pursuit of racial justice.

CHAPTER 2

NAVIGATING THE ISMS

Let's begin this journey of navigating how the myth of race turned into the reality of race, now that in the 21st century, it has penetrated every aspect of civil society. For the remainder of the chapter, we examine the world of isms. An ism is a distinctive doctrine, cause, or theory—think racism, feminism, or patriotism. All isms make assumptions/presumptions and define terms as they see them. They keep people separated and give one group power over another.

Whether consciously or subconsciously, our world revolves around isms. Most of society's issues are formed from misunderstandings and problems associated with isms and othering. **When power meets prejudice, the outcome is always oppression, the advancement of one group over another.** In today's society, we like to believe power and privilege have minor effects on the world we live in. Many are ignorant about how privilege, power, and the isms affect daily life.

RACISM

Racism is defined as prejudice, discrimination, or antagonism directed against someone of a different mythical race based on the belief that one's own mythical race is superior. As indicated in the introduction of this chapter, racism has existed in American society since the nation's birth. In fact, racism was an inherited trait that became a full-blown disease once greed and power took root. This country's foundation was scripted on racist ideology, and its past continues to haunt us today, 500 years later.

A racist is defined as a person who shows or feels discrimination or prejudice against people of other races or who believes that a particular race is superior to another. Racism includes any attitude, action, or social policy that subordinates someone based upon the person's skin color (Jones 1997; Ponterotto, Utsey, and Pederson 2006).

CALL TO ACTION

Remember my interactions with my first professor. Would that incident be based on racism? Would he be considered racist?

- Find a person of color (POC) that you work with, have a relationship with, or know personally. Go have coffee or tea with them. This is a great opportunity for a learning moment. Read the professor's scenario with them and ask them how they perceive this incident.
- Reread the definition of racism and see what your friend thinks. Talk about White body trauma and supremacy. Remember: if you are in the fight for racial justice, it takes work. You have to understand the role that racism plays in your life and slowly begin to detox yourself from its complex layers guiding the way you think and feel. Do it until you become comfortable talking about race.

Racism can be explicit or unconscious, but it always harms, discriminates, and offends. Racism has matured throughout the centuries so that now it can occur unconsciously or subtly, currently dubbed as unconscious or implicit bias (defined later). Although these are textbook definitions, they are applicable to countless interactions, both subtle and overt, that occur every day. And although many White people like to believe that racism does not exist, this belief is far from reality. In a 2016 article on the

Ben & Jerry's website it is stated that "when White people occupy most positions of decision-making power, POCs have a difficult time getting a fair shake, let alone getting ahead." Systemic racism shows up in wealth, education, healthcare, employment, police surveillance, criminal justice, and housing. It's these acts of discrimination, covert prejudice, hostility, and negative feelings that keep the cycle going.

Systemic racism has led POCs to live in a state of chronic oppression. Oppression is a social act of placing severe restrictions on an individual group or institution (Appleby, Colon, and Hamilton 2011). For some, it even involves interlocking systems of oppression. The oppressed are typically devalued, exploited, and deprived of privileges by those individuals or groups who have more power (van Wormer, Kaplan, and Juby 2014).

Institutionalized racism is normalized, at times legalized, and is rarely corrected. Because institutional racism is so embedded in laws and policies, it often seems unreasonable that POCs are fighting for equity. I hear White people say all the time, "What else do *they* want?" This type of comment immediately demonstrates to me that they do not understand their privilege. By not acknowledging one's privilege, White people demonstrate very subtle, often undetectable (albeit very present) acts of discrimination, covert prejudice, and negative impressions that keep the cycle of racism going. There are many White people who feel entitled because of what they have been able to accomplish in this country, without acknowledging that it was only possible because enslavement created generational wealth.

In *How to Be an Antiracist*, author Ibram X. Kendi (2019) states that an idea, action, or policy is either racist or anti-racist. Racist ideology contributes to the narrative that regards people of different races as inherently unequal. Anti-racists, on the other hand, try to dismantle that storyline. That being said, we fall into either category depending on what actions we support. Furthermore, racism is profitable and rooted in patriarchy as well as capitalism. Although there are many different forms of racism, the belief systems are similar. White people are superior; Black people are more physically dominant, violent, and threatening. It is this thinking that has shaped our society since the days of enslavement.

It is exactly this sort of mentality that caused me to have experienced one of the most stressful and emotionally taxing situations I have had to deal with. For the last decade, my behavioral health practice has been providing a variety of supportive services to a diverse community. Recent political tension caused division within the Board of Education, which, by the way, is made up predominantly of POCs. While this type of tension causes chaos and reduced civility, the most painful part was watching how it hurt the children in the district who are already vulnerable.

As the tension increased and various agendas began to unfold, my relationship with the district became fragile. First, it was related to a lack of data, fidelity, type of service, and so on, and this went on and on for months. Other contracts managed by our practice began to be questioned, my relationships with key stakeholders and decision-makers were highlighted, and the narrative quickly became that contracts were given to me because of my relationships with influential people. The newspaper had a field day with this story. Interestingly, small-city politics means that anybody who is anybody is targeted at some point or another. As a dear friend once told me, "this is the type of city that eats its young."

The public humiliation and character discrediting continued. The amount of money my company made was highlighted as if to insinuate that it was an excessive amount based on the services provided. This was a total contradiction to many of the small minority- and women-owned business initiatives that were underway throughout the city. I needed to take a moment to process how the story was being sensationalized. Here I was, a small business, growing in the city's procurement market, employing people, mostly of color, most of whom lived in and paid taxes back to the city, but somehow my business dealings were being narrated as suspicious at best.

The narrative became more vicious. Tensions grew between school officials and a newly formed parent advocacy group, led by a White woman, which began to demand school accountability. The local newspaper, led by a White editor who assigned a young White male journalist to cover this story, decided to pursue the piece and run with it. This period was difficult for many reasons. I fundamentally have a just-world belief system, starting with the idea that "good things happen to good people." Now, I know that is not true, but for me to have hope in humanity, I have to make that perspective one of my core values. I hired a crisis public relations (PR) person to help me with this situation. He was hired specifically because he was a White male, and challenging public scrutiny in the name of journalism is not one of my strong areas. I thought, "He will speak their language. We can settle this." I believe in conflict mediation and think there is always room for a middle ground. But the White newspaper editor was not interested in compromise. He had an agenda, and until he was finished with publicly challenging my credibility, he was not going to stop. I was one of many pawns of color in a much larger network to dismantle the mostly POC-led city.

Now, one could argue that this was a conspiracy theory. White privilege allows most White people to minimize the experience and pain of POCs. Another counter argument could be that plenty of White people get attacked by other White people in the newspaper. This is right. Reference the introduction; this is how White people have been socialized to deal with each other for centuries. When I spoke to the White editor in the presence of my PR person, he refused to stop running the story, without regard for the fact that it could destroy my practice, lead to unemployment for my staff, and leave hundreds of mostly Black and Brown children and their families who were receiving culturally competent treatment without services.

This story is the classic story of structural racism, as American as apple pie. There are countless White people who are billionaires because of the relationships they maintain, the circles that they run in, the lobbyists they pay, and the political contributions they make. And here I am operating under the system that White people created to be a successful entrepreneur and, clear as the day, Whiteness came and took it away. I was publicly shamed, made an example of, and exiled from the table. People, especially White people, told me that I needed to have thick skin. I heard this a lot. At the end of the day, that is not a game I am willing to play. It is toxic and nasty.

I did, however, try very hard to reach out to allies to gain support in ending this vicious cycle. Some did not respond, others shrugged it off as if it were not their responsibility, and a few called to express how unfair it was that I was being singled out (more on the differences in allyship in Part III). There was a basic acknowledgment that no other service provider, especially no one who was White, was questioned or targeted in the newspaper. Although I can appreciate the phone calls of those well-intended White people, this is not allyship.

Today's culture defines an ally as someone who aligns with and supports a cause with another individual or group of people. An ally is someone joined with another for a common purpose. There are many different types of allies, but for the purpose of this book, the focus is on White allies in the fight against racism. To some extent, White allies have assessed and acknowledged their privilege. Many times, White allies are considered as those who are "down" for POCs, and social media defines them as the "White woke." White allies tend to be in positions that they can educate others about the importance of inclusion, support creating diverse spaces, and effectuate change for marginalized groups. Many White allies believe that the world should be equitable and that structural racism has no place in our society.

Here is what allyship, living anti-racism, and supporting racial justice would look like regarding the preceding story:

1. An ally would write an opinion piece negating the false narrative. The person would send a powerful yet supportive letter to the editor expressing concern about the services that children of color in the district will not receive due to the conflict over the services provided by my diverse group of clinicians.

2. An ally in my profession would want to stand in unity, brokering a conversation on how to stop this damaging agenda. An ally would look at patterns of the number of POCs this paper has attacked and see if the paper's reporting had racist undertones.

3. An ally would provide emotional support and a plan of action on how to deal with their own people in a situation like this. Because after all, who knows how to navigate these waters best?

Unfortunately, none of that happened, but this time it was expected. I have learned to stand in my truth and for what I believe is right. This belief is embedded in the very fiber of who I am. Eventually, when all the dust settles, the truth, not the spin, not the sensationalized narrative, is the only thing that stands. Well-intended and supportive White people are not allies, and they do not have the right to claim allyship. If, as a White person, you are considering taking the necessary steps toward racial justice, a necessary first step is your readiness to take a bold stance against racism: look at it in the face, your own tribe, and dismantle it.

Another lesson I learned from this experience is that for White people, I was well suited to be a token, but with limits. I am light-skinned, highly educated, heteronormative, and married with kids. White support only goes as far as they need me to fulfill their quota, check their diversity box, and exploit my relationship with the community. But the moment I needed my "allies" to return the favor in kind, meaning that I am asking for the same amount that I give, it became none of their business and "something personal I need to deal with." How is this connected to White guilt? Well, I saw it every day when I was interacting with the well-intended White people who sat on the sidelines and watched.

PATRIOTISM VERSUS BIGOTRY

Patriotism is defined as the love of country and attachment to national values. The problem with the flag, the national anthem, and narratives of American patriotism is that they ignore the fact that America was, and is, a colonial state. Patriotism has never been a racially equitable experience because it was never designed to be. A patriot is an individual who loves, supports, and defends the country. A bigot, on the other hand, is an individual "who is strongly partial to one's own religion, race, or politics and is intolerant of those who differ," says the *American Heritage Dictionary* (n.d.). The difference between the two: patriotism is meant to be born out of love, whereas bigotry is born out of hate.

A big topic of debate in the past few years has been patriotism and whether it implies prejudice. Research shows that 72 percent of millennials of color believe the Confederate flag is a symbol of racism and they support removing Confederate statues and symbols from public places. In contrast, a majority of Whites (55 percent) see the Confederate flag as a symbol of southern pride and oppose removing Confederate statues and symbols. Group pride can certainly be empowering. But if it's taken the wrong way, it can evoke feelings of discrimination and prejudice. For example, following the September 11 attacks, national pride quickly turned into hostility toward the Muslim and Middle Eastern communities. This has increased significantly over the years due to bigotry in the name of patriotism, especially when it comes to elections. Although patriotism is supposed to be about "pride in country," it has now become synonymous with prejudice.

Group conflict shows that group pride is half of prejudice. During the 2008 elections, both bigotry and patriotism showed themselves to be true. Although the election had a favorable result, throughout the election process, bigotry was demonstrated in that President Obama's opponents often used his race against him and pinpointed his ethnicity as a reason why he would not be an effective president. Some questioned whether he was truly "American" and questioned his aspirations for this nation. They questioned his identity and ridiculed his middle name, calling him a terrorist. On the other hand, patriotism was clearly shown by the candidate's favorability and political engagement. It was this campaign that allowed for our first self-identified African American president. It also illustrated how both race/racism played critical roles in society as well as racist logic, narrow notions of patriotism, and national identity (Parker, Sawyer, and Towler 2009).

With a different spin, patriotism has played a role in the current political climate. The results of the 2016 election demonstrated that many fear a diverse nation and the possibility that POC would garner too much power or political control. The findings of a University of Massachusetts study show an increase in the outward demonstration of racial bias and illustrate an inherent fear or anger about perceived threats of increasing diversity (UMass Diversity Reports). This study furthermore demonstrates that anti-immigration sentiments have increased since Trump's election, particularly with the realization of population trends indicating the Latinx community is quickly becoming the majority within the United States. Evidence is clear that we have not moved to a post-racial era.

So, where do we draw the line between patriotism and bigotry? I support a theory that several Black Psychologists have positioned which may feel uncomfortable to read: for a portion of the White population, most of whom are in positions of power, it is the fear of White extinction that is driving the hate and divisiveness.

It's projected that by 2050, POCs will be the new majority in the United States and be in positions of power. White extinction is a fear that White people will lose both the political and economic gains they have reached since the days of enslavement. "White extinction anxiety" has led White supremacists to feel threatened that they will lose their status and influence. These fears were further exacerbated once the political climate became more divisive. An increase in anti-immigrant rants has created a subtle amount of fear concerning White people losing their privilege and dominance. It is this fear and anxiety that have led to harsher conservative political party positions. It is this fear of "White genocide" that is fueling the Identitarian mindset in White supremacists. Fueling the fear is the anticipation of the "Browning of America," characterized by a continued blurring of once distinct racial and ethnic divisions (Rodriguez 2003). Furthermore, many White people fear "racial mixing" because they believe that reproduction between people of different races weakens the White demographics within society and poses an imminent threat to the stability of the White construct.

The roots of this theory date back to the days of enslavement and plantation owners being afraid of a slave rebellion that could have led to a race war and could have wiped out the White population. This happened all over the Caribbean. One of the foundational reasonings for segregated schooling was to dismiss any opportunity for interracial intimacy that could be sparked in the classroom. This demonstrated the underlying fear of "mixed blood" being reproduced. Standards of beauty are determined by Whites for Whites, and POCs don't fit those standards. Southerners' discomfort with integration was rooted in their fear of the racial hierarchy becoming displaced (Magnuson-Cannady 2005). This was made obvious by making interracial marriages illegal. In Virginia, interracial marriage was illegal thanks to the 1924 Act to Preserve Racial Integrity. Until this marriage law was challenged, the state had full control over who could marry who. These anti-miscegenation laws were enacted to ensure the superiority of the White race for more than 300 years.

It wasn't until the civil rights era that people started to challenge that mindset. In *Loving v. Virginia* in 1967, the Supreme Court unanimously decided to invalidate state laws restricting interracial marriage due to their violating the 14th Amendment (Roberts 2014). This win was monumental because previously in Alabama, the court upheld racial classification and denied interracial marriage. It was not until recently, in 2000, that Alabama made interracial marriage legal.

The terror that a drop of Black blood would cause racial impurity and would eventually lead to White people losing their privilege and superior status in America is unfathomable, perpetuates fear, and fuels racism. Shifting demographics heighten White extinction anxiety and to prevent White America from becoming an endangered species, White supremacists look for ways to oppress the dominance of melanin, no matter the level of dehumanization involved.

The combination of these fears and anxiety often manifests as White rage. In *White Rage: The Unspoken Truth of Our Racial Divide*, author Carol Anderson, PhD (2016) contends that anger and resentment have fueled racism at every turning point in Black American history. White Americans have always derailed the progress of POCs since the days of "freedom" and emancipation. According to Dr. Anderson, White rage is the rebellion-like behavior that shows up for White people when POCs begin making strides and advances toward equality.

Some examples: after the court ruling of *Brown v. Board of Education* (1954), which allowed for school integration, Black students were met with bricks, mobs, and violence. Years later, a law (The Tax Credit Scholarship) was passed to allow and use tax dollars to fund racially exclusive private schools. White rage is demonstrated in the assassination of progressive civil rights leaders like Malcolm X, Martin Luther King Jr., and Medgar Evers by White supremacists out of fear and hatred. It was demonstrated again in Tulsa, Oklahoma, and the 1921 massacre of Black Wall Street. The Tulsa massacre showed that in spite of hundreds of years under the oppressive system of enslavement, if left alone, Black people could build and establish their own thriving communities without a need for handouts. It is unfortunate that during that era, similar to many other historical markers, White supremacists were unable to tolerate the idea that Black communities were capable of not just building and rebuilding but also taking care of one another in harmony and thriving.

Barack Obama's election led to the rise of stand-your-ground laws and police brutality. The requirements of photo identification in order to vote affected a plethora of POCs. In a speech given at the NAACP annual convention, General Eric Holder (2012) reported that it would, in fact, adversely affect more than 6 million Black voters because 25 percent of Black Americans lack a government-issued photo identification, compared to 8 percent of White Americans.

For every Black advancement, there is a White backlash. It is carried out by those who have access to courts, police, governors, and legislators. It is feigned as noble and honest decision-making when in actuality it is driven by racist motivations (Anderson 2016).

STORY

Kristine Brown, Nonprofit Case Manager
African American woman, adopted by White family

My relationship with White allies is full of mixed emotions. I've experienced positive and negative encounters with White people who thought they were allies. My views about allyship have been informed by being African American and adopted by a White family, having a Master of Social Work degree with over  15 years of working with diverse populations, being married to a Black man, and raising a Black son.

Being African American and adopted by a White family of Italian descent was an experience that has shaped my entire life. I grew up in a mostly White suburb and never saw people who looked anything like me, so at a young age, I began to feel like something was wrong with me. Why didn't I look like what was all around me? I was Brown-skinned and my hair was bushy and curly, and at that time I felt ugly. So, I needed to conform. I wanted to fit in and not stand out in any way. Being different was hard.

Thus began a lifelong battle with my self-esteem and self-worth. I loved my family but they could not give me what they didn't have. They didn't have the tools to raise a Black child. Perhaps what hurt the most is that they didn't even try. They didn't try to find Black dolls or playgroups with kids of color. They didn't try to befriend people that looked like me. They couldn't even be bothered with going to a Black salon to learn how to properly do my hair. Those are the basics so they certainly didn't know how to be an ally to my people. They refused to even admit it. When someone called me the N-word one day at school, instead of addressing it, they told me to tell people I was just a really tan Italian person. It would actually be funny if it didn't hurt so much. When relatives said I was too ugly to be in family pictures, they didn't advocate for my right to just exist. When strangers gave us looks or even asked why I was so dark, they immediately had to clarify that I was adopted.

Growing up with the absence of allies in my own home, I decided that advancing this cause as an adult would be my lifelong mission. After lots of therapy, cutting ties with toxic relatives, and learning who I was as a Black woman, I have come to love this work, believe this is vital, and believe it will ultimately benefit all Black and Brown folks. I have come to understand the power of being unapologetically Black, the beauty of our people, the painful history we have endured, issues of colorism, and structural racism, and the many challenges that we currently face.

I see the most important part of allyship for White people is having the courage to go into White spaces and confront openly racist acts and rhetoric as well as being aware of their own privilege and confronting others on theirs.

Here is a small yet significant example. A White friend of mine was on vacation in Georgia. She saw a man on the beach with a giant White supremacist tattoo. She went right up to him and engaged in a meaningful dialogue about his tattoo, politics, privilege, and so on. To me, that was brave and, really, what more people need to do when they see things like that man's tattoo. He may not change his stance on White supremacy, but as an ally, she engaged him in a deep conversation about race and challenged his beliefs. Meaningful, long-term, and sustainable change happens one interaction at a time. When allies like this engage, they help the larger cause of highlighting the hatred and creating dialogues to begin to address it, and they get other people to start thinking about it in the context of their own lives.

An ally can only be useful and/or helpful if that individual truly understands their motivations behind wanting to be in that role.

To advance or promote something that you support is noble, but I believe an ally needs to do it through introspective assessment as to what is driving this desire. Is it just supporting equal rights? Does that person have a child and/or spouse of color and they feel some sort of draw into making the world a better place? Whatever the reason, for an ally to be useful, they first need to understand their own motivation.

One of my main concerns with allies is the guilt-driven motivation. White guilt and looking at POCs as "victims" who need to be "helped" is something POCs find frequently with White people who claim they are allies. They don't even realize that White privilege has affected their views, and instead of confronting that, they hide behind allyship so they don't get called out. For example, I have heard White people say things like "I have Black friends, I watch Oprah, I am married to or date a POC, so I'm not a racist and I am automatically an ally." That is not how this process works. You can marry and/or date a POC and still be racist. Real introspective work on oneself must be done before you can claim allyship and/or advocate.

Furthermore, there are key characteristics an ally must have. A White ally should be insightful, brave, woke, and well educated on the Black struggle for equality from a historical perspective to the current state of affairs. They should have a wide-ranging knowledge of the vernacular and an understanding as to why Black people use the N-word and why White people cannot use the N-word. A White ally is someone who is also comfortable in Black spaces, has meaningful relationships with POCs throughout different facets of their lives, and can take on the task of challenging their own.

One of the most important things a White person should understand is that being a White ally is not just a trend. It is meant with the intention of creating meaningful conversations on behalf of those who are marginalized. It is living with the intention that whenever the opportunity presents itself, no matter how uncomfortable and challenging things get, they show up and elevate POCs. For example, there is a passage in Michelle Obama's (2018) book *Becoming* where she is reviewing résumés to bring in new associates to the law firm where she works. She brings up the point that if the firm wants to add more diversity, they need to cast a wider net to bring in talented POCs. If a White partner at her firm had said that, that would be an example of being a White ally.

A White ally means listening to our experiences, not minimizing but listening and honoring us. Talking about race is not always easy, but we need allies who are willing to let comfort go so that real change can begin. I feel that the more Black folks you know, the less likely you are to stereotype us. The less you stereotype us, the less likely you are to fear us. The less you fear us, the less likely you will want to hurt us.

An important fact that White people need to understand is that by saying they don't see color or that they are color-blind, they are engaging in a form of racism and putting their head in the sand when it comes to matters of race. We are not color-blind and we do not live in a color-blind world. Seeing color is good; seeing and emphasizing differences is a good thing. That is the whole point: we are different, and we should see each other as different and that is what we want. There is beauty in our differences and saying you are color-blind diminishes all POC experiences.

If you want to become a solid White ally, you must read about Black life, be in community with Black people, give us the benefit of the doubt, and understand us the way we must understand you. The importance of establishing racial literacy is crucial in these roles. Once you have gained awareness, then you need to school your White brothers and sisters, your cousins and uncles, your loved ones and friends, and all who will listen to you about the White elephant in the room: White privilege. They may not become as defensive with you, so you must be the ambassador of truth. Those of you who know better must tell other White people what you know. If you stay silent, then you are actually complicit in racial injustice persisting.

Finally, your participation in protests, rallies, and local community meetings makes a huge difference. When we gather to express grief, outrage, and dissent, your presence sends the signal that this is not just "a Black thing" but a human thing as well.

Here is a quote that I share with allies in my circle:

> *Your voices, White voices, are crucial because the doubt of Black humanity, the skepticism of Black intelligence, and the denial of the worth of Black bodies linger in our cultural unconsciousness. If you challenge White ignorance or indifference to the plight of people of color, it will lend our causes needed legitimacy.*
>
> —Tears We Cannot Stop: A Sermon to
> White America *by Michael Eric Dyson (2017, 208)*

CHAPTER 3

THE ROLE OF BIAS IN ISMS

Can we possess bias without being racist? Absolutely. I have had numerous open conversations with White people who possess biases, and at the same time, I would not consider them racist. I had a neighbor who operated in the world thinking that many Black people could not get out of their own way to be successful, the same way she had in order to get out of poverty. She had a biased view that Black people chose to be poor, lazy, and on public assistance. This bias did not make her think her Whiteness was superior to Black people, but it did activate her worldview about how she interacted with many of our Black neighbors and the Black kids in our neighborhood magnet school. When I invited her to a deep, meaningful conversation about our differences, she was able to share these thoughts that carried a lot of shame. I was able to give her resources to read, data to contradict her way of thinking, and other more advanced allies she could talk with to develop in her allyship. This is a hard concept for allies to understand. This chapter examines belief systems, values, and biases. If biases are allowed to dictate behaviors, attitudes, and actions, then isms are reinforced.

Belief systems are often constructed through our upbringing, experiences, and events that shaped our thought processes. It is these "experiences" that give us reason to justify why we think the way that we do and, inherently, why we treat people the way that we do. We are more willing to accept outcomes that match how we think. More often than not, it is this bias within our beliefs that overrides logical and rational thinking. And if you are familiar with how our thought processes impact our behavioral responses, then you should know that our belief system alters our decisions (Dube, Rotello, and Heit 2010). The pre-existing view and ingrained knowledge of our world become our everyday way of thinking and interacting with POCs. For example, African countries are shithole countries,

Mexicans are rapists, Black people are lazy, Muslims are terrorists, and so on. It is only by examining your belief systems that you are able to reconstruct them and begin the journey of allyship.

Similar to how belief systems are constructed, our values are established by our personal experiences, social environment, and culture. Our values determine the type of person we want to be, what is important to us, and what motivates us. People who are unconsciously or overtly taught to maintain their White privilege use these values to cover up their biased opinions (Greenberg 2015). For example, in some cultures, there is an underlying value that you have to work hard to get what you want. However, White people with this value often ignore or are blinded by the fact that many POCs work very hard, often twice as hard as their White counterparts, to achieve the same goals due to the disadvantaged position from where they began. This is where bias impacts values.

Our bias is our preconceived notion, belief, or feeling about something. It is often based on stereotypes that can lead to prejudicial actions and discrimination. It is when our brain takes in information and forms a generalized opinion. Additionally, cultural conditioning, media, and both belief systems and values play a part in how we maintain our biased thinking.

Let's contextualize this point. It is well documented that people with "ethnic"-sounding names are less likely to be hired than those with White-sounding names. Why? There is a historical stereotype that POCs epitomize laziness or incompetence. The disconcerting aspect of bias is that many POCs are not treated fairly because of a perceived cultural bias. I have heard White statements such as "Why would Shaniqua's mother give her that name? Didn't she consider how difficult it will be for her to get a job with that name?" Interestingly, this same White opinion does not apply to White parents who name their children after fruits, seasons, cities, or boroughs. There is a double standard here.

As an ally, one's responsibility is to challenge the status quo. Why is it that Shaniqua is going to have a harder time finding a job than Brooklyn or Apple? With all things being equal, if Shaniqua has the same level of education, the same work ethic, the same solid references, then she should have a fair shot at that position.

CALL TO ACTION

- Develop a growing awareness of how bias operates and actively work against it. Implement awareness accountability and involve POCs in this process. Integrate awareness training with regard to specific situations such as name discrimination.
- If you work for a predominantly White company, educate others about the role of bias in the hiring process and, if able, challenge the hiring practices to be more inclusive.
- Advocate for trainings, check-ins, and including a diversity hiring goal, therefore creating accountability around diversifying the work environment.
- Create a clear path toward inclusion efforts that open opportunities for POCs to be hired by or to advance in your company.

That said, in my opinion, diversity and inclusion jobs should be reserved for POCs, with White allies only taking those positions when there are no other options. White executive teams may call on and hire diversity firms to lead and "solve" their racism or bias problem without actually committing to real change. Diversity trainings should be geared toward addressing and challenging White privilege, implicit bias, and microaggression; White diversity leaders find themselves having to soften the message. For this reason, diversity facilitators, most of whom are White women, tackle these issues by prioritizing the comfort of White audiences instead of having open dialogues about how racism shows up in the workplace. Starbucks, Prada, H&M, and Dove are recent examples of this phenomenon.

CALL TO ACTION

- Ask yourself this: Why is it that Shaniqua's name is considered strange but a name like Apple isn't? Where did that perception begin, and why? Who does it benefit the most? What was your visceral reaction when you read these questions? Think about the double standard of Whiteness and superiority in this situation.

- Make a list of your beliefs (beliefs are our attitudes about something that we believe to be true without proof, e.g., trust, faith, or confidence in something or someone). Who taught you your beliefs? Where did you learn to think this way? Are you proud of your beliefs? Do you feel ashamed of your beliefs? It is important that you examine the origins of your beliefs if you are truly committed to becoming an ally. You must be willing to make adjustments to the way that you think to be effective in this work.

Furthermore, if you are in the racial/social justice world as an activist but have not appropriately deprogrammed, privilege says you are the best person to get POCs to the other side of their struggle. The inclination that comes from privilege is that you know better, and for that reason, your opinions matter more than those who are in a perpetual cycle of struggle and failure.

BIAS IN PUBLIC ISSUES: GUN VIOLENCE

Gun violence in urban communities is one of those controversial topics. Some White people discount the data for racial profiling in stop-and-frisk, arrest, and harsh sentencing practices by claiming that it is not the racist laws that are destroying communities of color. Instead, they claim that Black-on-Black crime and shootings are the culprits of the destruction. The data are clear about this: White people are the largest offenders of mass shootings, typically propelled by hate crimes. According to Statista research and Grant Duwe, 64% of public shootings have been conducted by white people (Duwe 2014). Gun manufacturers, run by White people, continue to lobby for soft gun laws, giving accessibility to deranged White people to go on killing sprees. Inner-city gun violence is just a fraction of the deaths in communities of color. But the media pushes this narrative because exposing the truth would mean exposing the underbelly of the intrinsic White supremacist network.

Most White people who engage in social justice work ignore this very important piece of information because it would mean that they have to confront a very ugly truth about their people. Dismantling gun violence by addressing White supremacy is core to changing senseless gun laws. In most situations, this is a less favorable choice, because when White people confront other White people on their racism, one's White privilege is at stake, one's White card may be removed, and one may be disinvited from the White table. So, instead, many allies decide to take the path of least resistance by committing their lives to saving poor Black and Brown kids who are killing each other in dangerous inner cities. They start or lead nonprofits in the name of justice while their own people continue to run amuck. What does it mean that instead of confronting the perpetrators who cause the problem, well-intentioned White people ignore this responsibility and leave that fight for POCs?

DEALING WITH BIAS: CODE-SWITCHING

One of the ways that a POC responds to these types of situations is by developing the ability to switch between cultures, something called code-switching. Originating from linguistics, as one's ability to switch between languages, code-switching has now become a mainstream way to transition between White-appropriate identity and our authentic racial identity with ease (Auer 2005). Why is code-switching an important skill for Black people to learn?

White privilege affirms for White people that they can discredit the need to learn code-switching, even when entering into diverse/ urban neighborhoods, educating diverse kids, working with diverse families, and mentoring diverse youth. The proper protocol and consideration for entry into diverse communities are often overlooked and disregarded. In fact, it is likely that most White people have an expectation that everyone should conform to White social norms because privilege tells you that White is right; it is the "dominant" or "majority" culture that needs to be followed, and everything else is wrong. POCs conform to White norms for survival reasons, not because they are better or superior.

My husband and I taught our children to code-switch from a very early age. When they were as young as two or three years old, my children began code-switching training. If they were attending a prestigious, mostly white, educational program or private school, we would put them in inner-city sports leagues, dance/art classes, and summer camps. We taught them how to present themselves among White people and how they needed to transition without so much as blinking when they were around their kinfolk. Every so often, they would forget to switch, and they thought they could speak in the same tone that Mckenzie spoke to her mom or dad, but we reminded them quickly that they needed to remember to code-switch. We taught code-switching as a learned behavior used in order to survive—and succeed—in a White environment. Being intentional about teaching our children these skills allowed them to be accepted by many of their White peers. They would hear comments like "You are not really Black; you are different; you are actually smart." Comments such as these are microaggressions, by the way!

Being intentional also taught them not to delude themselves into thinking that because we taught them how to code-switch, which garnered White acceptance, that they were given a White pass or would, in any way, gain White privileges. POCs have had to learn to be bi-, tri-, and multicultural whether we wanted to or not. Those who thrive in White spaces are master code-switchers.

POCs are aware of how uncomfortable and suspicious White people feel when we act too Black or congregate together for too long. I can't tell you how many times I have been in a large gathering and found myself in a smaller group of POCs when, inevitably, a White person comes into the circle and says something like "Boy, it looks like you guys are having fun!" That is a microaggression because what most White folks in this situation are really thinking is, "Let me see what these colored people are conspiring about." In those moments, POCs recognize your privilege and power. Do you?

Privilege tells you that it is perfectly OK to enter communities of color and tell them what to do. You are, by birthright, the true decision-maker, and your solutions are worth more than gold because you can fix what you perceive to be broken. The colonizer mindset takes over as automatic as breathing. It is important to recognize that when White people are invited into communities of color, it is a privilege, and there is a protocol that must be followed. Most White people do not take the time to understand or follow the protocol, and their entitlement overrides the cultural norms that have been established by the POC village.

White people do not like to feel uncomfortable. Taking on the systems created to benefit White people is not a feel-good decision. Nonetheless, the ultimate truth is that the problem of racism lies with White people, so solving the problem requires White people to look at themselves and change themselves and the other White people around them.

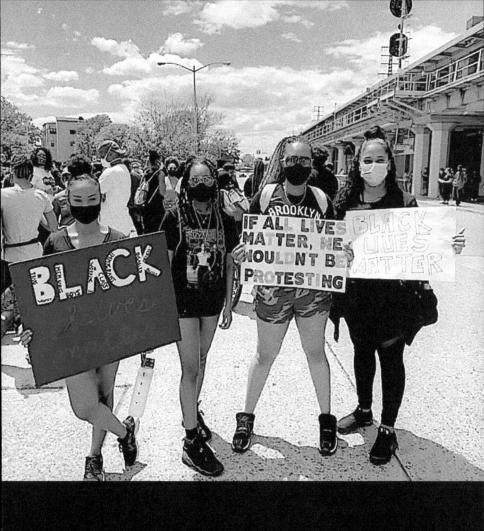

CHAPTER 4

UNCONSCIOUS/
IMPLICIT BIAS

Unconscious or implicit biases are social stereotypes that individuals form outside their conscious awareness. As described earlier, to be biased is to have and display unfair favor of one thing over another. What is important to understand about implicit bias is that once you are aware it exists, it is no longer implicit or unconscious. At the point that one continues to operate from a place of bias, it becomes a willful choice to do so, whether one believes it or not. Biases are not limited to ethnicity and race; they also include age, gender, sexual identity, and religion, among others. But race is the focus of this book, so that is what our conversation is centered on.

From a social sciences perspective, unconscious bias makes all the sense in the world, and it also gives White people a pass. By peeling back the layers of indoctrination around unconscious bias, there exists a slippery slope that moves you closer to practicing covert racism if you are not careful and aware. Unconscious or implicit bias negatively impacts interactions with POCs because biases are often apparent in the form of body language, awkward conversations, patronizing comments, nonverbal signals, and tension. The real truth is that unconscious or implicit bias reinforces structural and systemic racialization. It creates barriers that hinder access to opportunities. These unconscious biases are more often than not accompanied with microaggressions.

Microaggressions are brief and subtle insults or messages directed toward people of color (POCs) either intentionally or unintentionally. They communicate a certain level of distrust, fear, or negativity. Although not conscious, they stem from deeply rooted systemic bias, privilege, and oppression, and inequities in power (Dovidio et al. 2002; Sue 2003). Microaggressions cause POCs to feel excluded, untrustworthy, abnormal, and targeted. Studies show that racial microaggressions have a harmful impact on the recipients physically, emotionally, cognitively, and psychologically. Other symptoms include stress, low self-esteem, suicidal ideations, alienation, negative thoughts, and anger, among others. Multiple microaggressions, over time, can build up and lead to an intense traumatic impact generationally (Constantine and Sue 2007). This shows up as microinsults or microinvalidations that communicate a negative demeanor toward POCs (Sue, Capodilupo, and Holder 2008). Microinvalidation occurs when your side of the story is dismissed or minimized and you are made to feel that you don't know what the rules are in addition to being construed as being too sensitive. It is the behavioral or verbal expressions that convey shock when a Black student is told that they speak so "eloquently" or when statements are made that "All Lives Matter" when criticizing Black Lives Matter.

Microaggressions are particularly infuriating because most White people will not acknowledge that they are microaggressing when confronted. Instead, the POC is left feeling as though they are overreacting or angry for no reason. Recognizing that "the diversity thing" is in vogue right now, what is the point of having training on microaggressions or implicit bias for the purposes of diversity and inclusion initiatives if it does not translate to behavioral change and the work/school/organizational culture continues as it is? **Not acknowledging microaggressions as racism breeds a lack of accountability and gives White people a pass.**

Here is an example. Some time ago, I visited a local spa in my neighborhood. Every month, this spa used discount coupons as a marketing tool to entice customers to buy or add-on services. Interestingly, the checkout receptionist, a young White woman, always seemed to get annoyed when I showed her my discount email.

She would examine the email for expiration dates, name, address, and type of service for which the discount could be applied. I never saw her do this with any of the White customers, which gave rise to my suspicion that something was not quite right.

Despite the checkout drama, I continued to go to this spa. If I overlooked the attitude of the receptionist, services by the technicians were pretty good, and it was a great place to relax. Yet I was conflicted about continuing to patronize this establishment because this one person made the experience negative for me. Remember, POCs often do not immediately attribute awkward interactions with White people to racism. It is only through a great deal of deliberation, consultation, and courage that we make the call.

I really could not put my finger on the visceral reaction I was having with this White woman and did not connect the dots that microaggressions were at play. So, I thought to myself, maybe it's just me, I am being too sensitive. Until the moment—there is always an awakening moment that happens with POCs—that crystallized the realization of, I am not being too sensitive.

During my next appointment, I patiently sat in the waiting area until the White woman before me was ready to pay. At that moment, I felt anxious about showing my coupon because I knew the White receptionist was going to give me an attitude. I watched closely to see how she was going to handle the woman who was checking out before me, having earlier peeked at her phone while she was scrolling to find her coupon. Then I saw the unthinkable. During the checkout, as expected, the White woman sitting next to me showed the discount email. The White receptionist said, "Yes, we will gladly apply the discount, and did you know that we have a VIP membership that is free where you will accumulate points and every sixth service will be free?"

My blood began to boil. I was already on edge and pure rage consumed me. This is the physical manifestation of people who have to absorb White microaggressions, daily, hourly, all the time. I could not believe it. I had been given an attitude for the past year by this woman about using my coupon and she never told me about the VIP membership, which had been in existence since the prior year! I didn't even know what to do with myself. Do I stay; do I go; do I confront her and risk making a scene? No, no, don't do that; they will label you angry; you will perpetuate stereotypes.

I decided I would speak to the manager.

Suddenly, my task became explaining implicit bias and micro-aggressions to another clueless White person. The White manager tried to justify why the White receptionist had to examine my discounts and that she should do it with everyone. At that point, I went tone-deaf and only heard, "Blah, blah, blah, I will do nothing about this, but thanks for coming and we will take your money as long as you keep tolerating our bullshit." You get the gist of the story.

Here is how this situation could be handled completely differently by the manager.

CALL TO ACTION FOR THE WHITE MANAGER

1. Acknowledge the complaint. Do not dismiss it, do not justify the behavior, and do not act as if it did not happen. If you are in the service industry, understand that as long as a customer is not being abusive, they are always right.

2. Take the complaint seriously and call it what it is. You may not know it is a microaggression, but you will certainly know that the customer felt wronged or invalidated.

---

3. Consider your corrective options, including a verbal warning or a write-up for the receptionist. Consequences bring about change.

4. Educate your staff on the principles of diversity and inclusion and provide training in this area (more on this topic later). Enact organizational monitoring and change so that the spa becomes a more inclusive place for all people. This is particularly important because of the 1.2 trillion dollars that communities of color spend on consumer goods. In fact, in the health and beauty industry alone, it is estimated that Black shoppers spend $473 million in total hair care and $127 million in grooming aids (Nielsen 2018). Nielsen's 2019 Diverse Intelligence Series Report stated that POCs spend nearly nine times more than our non-Black counterparts on beauty and hair products. So POCs, more so than White people, drive the health and beauty industry.

5. Offer a kind gesture. "We see that you have been a loyal customer for the past year and have had five services with us. We will immediately enroll you in our VIP program and give you credit for the free sixth session. Dr. Akbar [not Maysa mispronounced], today's service is free. We value you as a customer." This type of response applies not just to the concept of allyship in support of diversity; it's also just good customer service.

Now about the White lady in the waiting area. Is she just an innocent bystander?

STORY

Dr. Noel Casiano, Clinical Psychologist
Latinx, author, husband, and father

As I share my story about allyship, it is unfortunate and sad to recognize that I personally do not have an example of a White ally in my lifetime. There have been many White people that I thought were White allies, but when they had to cross that threshold to truly be considered a White ally, I was disappointed either from their actions or decisions.

I have experienced situations in which even when I had more experience and better job qualifications, I was passed over by a White employer or hiring manager for a fellow White person. While I thought that this White person was an advocate for me as a Puerto Rican man, I was surely disillusioned and hurt in the process. In a social context, during a presentation, another person who I thought was a possible White ally overlooked publicly highlighting my educational achievements and doctoral degree in clinical psychology. By this action of unconscious bias, that person took away my credibility in front of a White audience and minimized what could have been a scholarly discourse into a laissez-faire chat.

I could continue to recount the many missed opportunities of individuals who would consider themselves to be White allies but failed to rise to the occasion due to their White privilege. Mostly, what I have witnessed are so-called White allies who are motivated by front-facing or photo ops rather than standing side by side in solidarity with a particular culture or marginalized group.

Despite these experiences, I am clear on what the journey can look like for White people who are genuinely invested in helping communities of color. They can either be advocates or allies through my lens of the world we live in. I think being either can bring up mixed thoughts and emotions. Advocates, depending on their personal history, can respond to and experience this role in many different ways. An advocate is a person who can speak or write in favor of another person or a worthy cause and even support a specific cause by their personal action no matter the consequence to their person. This is what I like to call a First-Person Advocate.

A Second-Person Advocate is someone who supports a person or a movement but will not advocate with personal investment. A Second-Person Advocate may write letters, send emails, and/or sign a petition but will not be seen in the public square, risking

CALL TO ACTION
FOR WHITE LADY IN THE WAITING AREA

- Meet with a POC in the service industry. Talk this scenario through with them. Share this story with them. Ask them their opinions and how you could be an advocate in that moment.

Ask them:

- How should the White lady in the waiting area have intervened? If she overheard my complaint, what should she have done?

Now, your turn:

- If that were you, what would you have done?
- Are you afraid to speak up? If so, why?
- How could you demonstrate allyship in that moment?

in-person consequences. In other words, a First-Person Advocate can be an active participant in a specific cause or movement while a Second-Person Advocate can be involved in a specific cause or movement but in a more passive manner. I can see how both First and Second Person advocacy can be positive, but the First-Person Advocate is risking more and showing a deeper sense of advocacy.

The word *ally* now has a more personal and intimate meaning. An ally is a person who will unite emotionally, psychologically, and even physically to a person or cause. An ally has a close connection to a person or mutual cause because of shared values, morals, philosophies, and overall worldview. This alliance brings the ally to move toward an action or achieve goals or desired outcomes. Allies will also share what I like to call an "emotional ecosystem" that unites them in seeking positive systemic results that will allow them to have a sense of positive feelings, well-being, and justice for humanity. This overall cooperation in their friendship, organization, and/or movement will keep their allied connection closely bonded together, no matter the circumstance or even individual consequences.

I want to address what I consider to be a good White ally. A good White ally has to have a deep, honest, and personal conviction that they want to partner with another culture to have a sense of association and connection to that culture. This type of ally must have a solid understanding of the cultural history, norms, and values of the culture as well as a respect for diversity.

A good White ally will advocate for the well-being of that culture without taking over the culture's voice. A White ally will also provide information and resources that the other culture has not had access to. A White ally will have a deep association with that culture by standing up against racist undertones or overt racial discrimination. A White ally will risk their own personal advancement for the protection and inclusion of that culture from the more dominant group. Last, a White ally will communicate clearly and not speak for the culture unless it is in collaboration with this culture. Allies understand, see, and fight against racial injustice every single day on whatever platform they frequent, public or private. Instead of White allies having to do this on their own, ideally, they should recruit other White people to join them in the process. Bringing in the reinforcements makes allyship statements more impactful.

PART II
DECONSTRUCTING
WHITENESS

<   **Thread**

mi
@helloalegria

white people find the term "white
people" uncomfortable because
they're used to being the default
definition of "people".

1:34 PM · 9/2/17 · Twitter for iPhone

60.8K Retweets **174K** Likes

CHAPTER 5

WHITE PRIVILEGE

Disclaimer: This chapter may be uncomfortable due to the severity of issues and topics discussed. You may find the concept of allyship demanding or critical of the work that has already been done by self-proclaimed allies. We all hold different levels of power. People have many identities, and this is complicated. For that reason, it is important to recognize the limitations of this book in that Whiteness/White people as defined can be seen as binary, meaning that it does not take into account the infinite number of subtle variations in White identity. Another limitation is that the book defines White as someone with White skin and White privilege and based on not being a person of color (POC). In addition, the construct of White in the context of this book is undifferentiated by religion, socioeconomic status, ethnicity, education, or any other characteristic. I recognize that intersectionality for identity exists. White people also contend with many aspects of their identity, and for this reason, it is understandable that choosing the identity that means the most to you will be more important than material advantage and will often dictate how one responds to situations involving privilege or lack thereof. Furthermore, the term is not used to discriminate or cause an "othering" perception, but it is meant to target how the White construct has been used to elevate a specific group of people.

It is also important to acknowledge that my approach of deconstructing terms and ideology that further feed oppression, racism, and inequality that exist for POCs may seem unhelpful in building strong alliances or pursuing racial justice. With that in mind, please see this book not as a demand but rather as an invitation to use this information to examine your process. This is not an attack but an opportunity to learn. And openness to learning is the most important position you can take as someone wanting to be an ally.

DEFINING WHITE PRIVILEGE

White privilege is the societal advantage White people have just for identifying as White and not as a racial minority. It is unearned entitlement, unearned power, and unearned advantage (McIntosh 1989). It is this same privilege that allows White people to go into a store and easily find clothing or makeup that matches their shape or their skin tone. It's the ability White people have to turn on the television and see people who look, speak, and act the same as they do. White citizens have the ability to function knowing that their needs are generally met almost immediately. POCs move through the world grappling with the notion that their needs may or may not be met. Their needs are met on a case-by-case basis. It's the financial, academic, and societal advantage White individuals have compared to POCs. White privilege is embedded in our history in the United States.

White privilege is anchored in systemic racism and biases, which continue to reproduce racial inequality. Before the Civil Rights Act of 1964, White privilege had both legal and systemic advantages, such as citizenship and voting rights. More specifically, during the civil rights era, White privilege was represented by the advantage of segregation. Many Whites are not even conscious of their relationship to power and privilege.

Presently, White privilege is present in almost every aspect of our society. Some of the most detrimental threats to diverse communities are the criminal (in)justice system, addiction/substance abuse, and housing/real estate.

CRIMINAL JUSTICE

Racial profiling, disproportionality in minority contact by law enforcement, harsher sentencing, higher rates of arrest, sentencing, and incarceration, by design, reinforce the notion of inferiority.

White privilege shows itself in the general disregard for Black and Brown bodies as it relates to teenagers, crime, and law enforcement. White privilege means that a White adolescent can roam about without fear that they will be a target or that their life is compromised simply because of the color of their skin, the clothes they wear, or the music that they listen to. It means that White teens can make mistakes and then be given an opportunity to correct them. For teenagers of color, White privilege looks like young Black boys, ages 15 to 19, who are 21 times more likely to be shot and killed by the police than young White boys (Equal Justice Initiative 2014). POCs are three times as likely as Whites to be searched and twice as likely to be arrested following a stop-and-frisk (The Sentencing Project 2018). Many authors have noted that Black boys as young as five years old are feared, and as a result of this fear, ill-trained police officers shoot first and ask questions later. Black people are less than 13 percent of the U.S. population, and yet they are 31 percent of all fatal police shooting victims, and 39 percent of those are killed by police even though they were *not* violent offenders (Federal Bureau of Investigation n.d.). White privilege is when police officers are not held accountable for murder and walk away freely or go on paid administrative leave. White privilege is when police protect and serve White citizens, rather than harass them. White privilege is the fact that the majority of our evening news reports are about urban crimes, but very few news stories cover the suburbs or urban crime that involve White men.

White privilege is also when police respond to absurd 911 calls such as #BBQBecky, #PermitPatty, and #CornerstoreCaroline (these hashtags describe social media's way of calling out White people who have irresponsibly dialed 911 on POCs for looking "suspicious" or otherwise engaging in everyday normal activities). White privilege is when POCs face longer sentences for lesser crimes while Whites receive shorter sentences for greater crimes. In fact, White male criminals are 5 percent more likely to be hired than a man of color with a clean record (NAACP n.d.).

Finally, media images of Black and Brown people are frequently criminalized to reinforce White privilege and White power. For insance, there are some White people presenting as allies, now and historically, who have shown up to rallies and initiated or contributed to looting. This act of looting is then captured by the media to further perpetuate the narrative that Black and Brown people are criminals, savages who do not know how to peacefully protest. Many White people agree that Black lives matter, but contradict this statement by saying they cannot support the looting and destruction of property. What is interesting about this statement is the hypocrisy. While these same White people remain silent about how exactly they will fight racial inequities, they are vocal about looting. While these same White people participate in the patriarchy that reinforces their privilege, they will judge the actions of the looters, which data show are mostly perpetrated by White out-of-towners anyway (Scher 2020). White privilege allows White people to sit from a place of judgement about the destruction of property and the theft of merchandise (which is replaceable), while they will not admit to the lands that their ancestors have stolen, pillaged, or burned down and the thousands upon thousands of POCs who have been murdered due to racist ideology.

SUBSTANCE ABUSE

White privilege was the war on drugs and the crack epidemic in communities of color that has now spun as the opioid crisis because White folks are overdosing. White privilege is pouring millions of dollars and resources to create mental health facilities where each White addict is treated with dignity and provided with a strong intervention/treatment plan. White privilege is criminalizing Black and Brown people who suffer from substance abuse and addiction. White privilege is when POCs are more likely to be arrested for drug offenses despite using drugs at a similar rate to White people. In fact, Black youth are 10 times as likely to be arrested for drug crimes than White youth (Rovner 2016). Drug possession and drug selling happen across all racial and socioeconomic groups; however, law enforcement concentrates on low-income urban areas. Whites are often under-arrested and set free from legal charges. Nearly 80 percent of people in federal prison and almost 60 percent of people in state prison for drug offenses are Black or Latino. The incarceration rate for African Americans tripled between 1968 and 2016 and is more than six times the White incarceration rate alone (Drug Policy Alliance 2016).

REAL ESTATE/HOUSING

White privilege is redlining and gentrification. Since being granted freedom, African Americans have been fighting for the lands they slaved over. The Homestead Act of 1862 was created to "give free African Americans" the chance to acquire land. However, certain White Southerners put legal obstacles in place to prevent ex-slaves from acquiring property (Shanks 2005). It is estimated that over 1.6 million White people, both immigrants and American-born, received free land and profited from that wealth, thus establishing a foundation of generational wealth. Years later, the Naturalization Act of 1790 became the first law in the United States granting national citizenship to "free White persons of good character." This again excluded POCs and made it difficult for them to obtain land and establish themselves as rightful citizens of the United States. The majority of the freed enslaved or immigrants of color had nothing to build on, which led to the present-day struggles POCs encounter when trying to break the cycle of poverty. The outcome of the Homestead Act is another example of policies resulting in racialization, economic detours, and sedimentation of racial inequality that shape the disparity of wealth between POCs and White people (Oliver and Shapiro 1995).

Redlining gave way for housing discrimination to continue. People of color continue to face housing discrimination at 45 percent while only 5 percent of White people report discrimination (Solomon, Maxwell, and Castro 2019). White privilege is when White people are shown housing in more prestigious areas, whether they can afford it or not, whereas POCs are shown housing in areas they can presumably "afford" or where they'd be "better off." When it comes to homeownership, just 41 percent of Black families own their own home compared to 73 percent of White families. The typical White household has 10 times more wealth than POC households (Shin 2015). White privilege is when financial flexibility through mortgages and loans is extended automatically to White people whereas POCs have to earn it.

Housing discrimination has been amplified in the last decade through gentrification. Gentrification is the displacement of POCs from the neighborhoods that they grew up in. It is characterized by an influx of wealthy White residents entering predominantly Black and Brown neighborhoods, driving the prices of housing and causing a strain on community members, many of whom have lived there for generations. In Washington, D.C. the percentage of Black residents declined from 71 percent to 48 percent due to gentrification while the percentage of White residents increased 25 percent and displaced more than 20,000 Black residents. Gentrification has become the new colonialism as the repercussions have inflated the economy and limited access to public health (Valoy 2014). Therefore, gentrification is more than just "beautifying" urban neighborhoods; it's another systemic and institutionalized way to displace POCs. Gentrification is when urban projects and residences are torn down with a commitment from local government to replace them with better housing and neighborhood life for residents. Or when universities expand their campuses into "undesirable" city locations and push the residents out of their neighborhood. So, when driving through this "newly developed neighborhood," consider how many POCs were displaced and disenfranchised as a result.

Historically, White flight occurred when POCs moved into urban centers. Interestingly, as White millennials and Gen Xers move into those same urban centers due to accessibility, ease of public transportation, and proximity to jobs, the same areas their parents and grandparents fled from, it is leaving an entire population of POCs disenfranchised and homeless. My hometown of Brooklyn, New York, is a perfect example of this phenomenon. Gentrification is also when businesses begin to cater to the newer White residents and even force some of the neighborhood staples to close because they are unable to compete with new local investors. Gentrification changes the entire vibe within a community. So yes, although investing in urban neighborhoods may seem like the best thing to do, think about the POCs who are already publicly invested in their neighborhood. Those residents are often portrayed as "criminals" when the newcomers start to feel unsafe. It is a profit-driven cultural shift generally fueled by White privilege.

Criminal (in)justice, substance abuse, housing—the list goes on and on.

There are also subtler ways in which White privilege shows up. White privilege is often characterized by entitlement and agency. Most White people, particularly in predominantly White spaces, demonstrate a commanding presence, esteem, and security that they are in their rightful place. As a result of White privilege, it is uncommon for a White person to feel that they are not good enough by virtue of their White identity group. It is uncommon to see a White person, even those with a lower education and socioeconomic status, act like they are not good enough or they do not belong. Even when entering spaces where POCs reside, the conqueror mentality kicks in immediately. As mentioned in the first chapter, colonizing is connected to White trauma. For these reasons, White people do not feel compelled to learn the operational rules of entering into spaces of color, while for POCs, learning to shift between cultures is standard operating procedure.

CALL TO ACTION

Now that you have recognized the important role of White privilege, how do you use it to support racial justice?

- Do you accept that White privilege exists?
- Name three ways that White privilege has helped you in your life.
- Now using those three scenarios, how do you know that White privilege gave you the advantage? How does it feel to know you have this privilege?
- List three things that you will do in the next month to support racial justice work.

The true power behind privilege lies in recognizing and admitting its ability to provide opportunities and advancement in our society. It is the true form of affirmative action on steroids. Still don't believe me? Jane Elliot, a tremendous ally in the fight for racial justice, once addressed an audience full of White people, proclaiming that if they did not believe in White privilege then they would have no problem trading places with a Black person. She asked the audience to raise their hand if they were serious about trading places. Not *one* person in that room raised their hand. She demonstrated that the audience was aware of the difference: they knew of their White privilege, they used it, and they did not want to give it up.

I repeated this same exercise in an Urban Trauma workshop just a few months back, with hundreds of White people in the room. The response was exactly the same. Not one single White person in the room raised their hand.

White people will argue that many "minorities" are looking for a handout, like affirmative action, and they fail to be accountable for the many ways in which they try to beat the system. Andre Perry, a fellow at Brookings Institution in Washington, D.C., whose work focuses on educational inequities, stated, "If the current college admissions scandal rocking the country tells us anything, it is that affirmative action is still needed" (Strauss 2019). The news broke in March 2019 that exposed White privilege and hypocrisy at the center of this scandal. Essentially, the White elite had paid millions to secure admissions for their children into high-ranking and Ivy League universities. The double standard is that these kids were admitted without raising doubt that they deserved to be there using fake sports scholarships and no follow-up on whether they belonged. Had these kids been Black or Brown students, those students' legitimacy in an Ivy League school would have been questioned immediately, very much like in my situation with the White male psychotherapy professor in graduate school.

White privilege can be challenging for White people who are unsure of how to go about having uncomfortable conversations. For some, they choose to remain "color-blind" to alleviate the feelings of guilt, anxiety, and shame that come with admitting to their White privilege. Work against this urge. It is not a productive way to manage awareness. Color-blindness does not and cannot exist in a racist society, and in fact, the very idea of color-blindness makes POCs feel unseen. The sad reality is that everyone else sees the color, accent, and physical attributes of a POCs. Those are distinguishing attributes. It is important to dispel the narrative of color-blindness because color has been long weaponized for White advantage. So, in supporting racial justice, see it for what it is, lean into it, teach other

White people about it, correct it when you see it, and be the voice of change in the White community.

INTERSECTIONALITY: WHITE PRIVILEGED AND POOR

Michelle Alexander (2020), in her book *The New Jim Crow: Mass Incarceration in the Age of Colorblindness*, expressed the notion that White people who believe in racial hierarchy thrive off the backs of poor Whites, and have for centuries (I chronicle the origin of this in the White Trauma section in Chapter 1). Many of them do not understand the true agenda of White supremacists but want to preserve their status/privilege and the little bit of financial stability that they do have.

I wanted to take special care to speak directly to those White people who grew up poor and don't buy the idea that White poverty comes along with certain entitlements. Even when faced with poverty, White people still maintain a state of privilege compared to POCs. Those who are in poverty will still receive a better hand than Black people, often believing themselves to be better than even the most educated, poised, and intelligent POCs simply because Whiteness is empowered and reinforced in every single part of society.

It is a myth that poor White people do not experience privilege. The fact is that class does not cancel out racial privilege. The White poor are still above Black people on the racial hierarchy (DiAngelo 2006). You can be separated by class but still connected by race. So, when it comes to shedding light on privilege, the White poor will try to dismiss racism by pointing to an area in their life where they are oppressed. However, in a White-dominant society, intersectionality can be complicated. For instance, economically poor White people are, in fact, marginalized in comparison to other White people from middle- or upper-class backgrounds. In some ways, poor Whites struggle and are at a disadvantage but in a very different way than POCs. If you fall or have fallen in this category, you may bear a huge resistance to privilege because oftentimes poor Whites have little or no experience with POCs and therefore may see themselves at the bottom of the heap when compared to the White middle class or White elite.

Intersectionality says that people may experience privilege in some ways but not in others. Most often, White privilege has more authority than class. White people exist in this world with unearned privileges through the development and sustainability of Whiteness which has become their birthright (Crosley-Corcoran 2014). Peggy McIntosh (2007), in "White Privilege: Unpacking the Invisible Knapsack," explores how White people are born with an advantage that even poverty cannot take away. The most common defensive position of most White people who are in poverty is "How can you say I have privilege when I've been discriminated against and called White trash?" The answer is simple. Your suffering is different. You have more opportunities than what you may know because of your White-skin privilege.

Most poor White people are not subject to bias in law enforcement and the criminal justice system or killed at a young age for looking suspicious. White skin is not weaponized like skin with melanin. White people do not have hashtags or a running list of individuals who have been gunned down or killed due to police brutality. White skin gives you the opportunity to live freely and actually make it out of poverty. Being poor does not erase your privilege or put you in the same category as Black people. Even if the term *privilege* sounds uppity, there is still a racial advantage, or "White priority," no matter your financial status. White people cannot dismiss the problem of racism by turning to socioeconomic class. Or as W.E.B. Du Bois once said, there are psychological and public gains associated with Whiteness (Sullivan 2017). Financial burdens may make things challenging, but your life is not made harder because of your Whiteness. Poverty does not cancel out privilege.

CALL TO ACTION

Reference history about the land given to European immigrants when they arrived in the United States. American society has catered to providing opportunities for Whites and, in turn, oppressing POCs.

- How has being White been an advantage, even if you are poor or working class? Think about how you live your daily life and try to imagine what that might be like if you were a POC. How would you be treated differently? In the job market? Access to education? In housing or real estate?

If you are reading this, it is because you are on the right side of White folks who do not believe in racial superiority based on one's degree of melanin. If you are reading this, it's because you need a road map and you want to get it right. If you are reading this, even the deepest indoctrination can be challenged if you are intentional about being a catalyst for change, rooted in freedom and justice for all people.

OPPRESSION OLYMPICS: THE UNFORESEEN OUTCOME OF PRIVILEGE

Now that we understand that privilege comes with power, it is not surprising, but still disappointing, that in the midst of efforts to dis-mantle racism, Whites and some non-Black POCs who have adopted White identity would engage in a competition about who is more oppressed, as if it were a battle that needs to be won. The Oppression Olympics is a competition to determine the weight

---

of oppression of individuals or groups, often by comparing race, gender, socioeconomic status, or disabilities (Francis 2016). This competition is set in order to determine who is worse off and the most oppressed. Some say that the Oppression Olympics exist because of the desire to one-up other victims and remain blind to the plights and disadvantages of different groups. It often comes across as a personal attack discounting the full range of a POC's experiences and placing one's own struggle ahead of that person. In any fight against any oppression, playing the Oppression Olympics is harmful; in the context of anti-racism work, it's very harmful because it creates the sense, over and over again for POCs, that White people have to win at everything, even oppression.

Bette Midler, a White woman, is a perfect example of someone who shone a light on how the Oppression Olympics is executed. She released a tweet after the Brett Kavanaugh investigation amid political strife and the testimony of Christine Blasey Ford. Despite claims of Kavanaugh's sexual misconduct highlighted by Dr. Blasey Ford's strong testimony, his Supreme Court nomination was passed to the Senate the very next day, with majority approval confirming his appointment just a few weeks later. Here was Bette Midler's reaction:

> *"Women, are the n-word of the world."*
> *Raped, beaten, enslaved, married off, worked like dumb animals; denied education and inheritance; enduring the pain and danger of childbirth and life IN SILENCE for THOUSANDS of years They are the most disrespected creatures on earth.*
> —Bette Midler

Black Twitter and every social and racial justice advocate and ally confronted Bette Midler via social media about her racially insensitive tweet. After quickly deleting the tweet, she sent out an apology stating her recognition of how her choice words were enraging to Black women and said she was an ally. Rooted in her privilege, Bette Midler probably did not realize that her comments minimized the dehumanizing treatment and systemic oppression that Black women and men have endured for centuries. Let's unpack the layers of this tweet, as it may not be immediately apparent why it was so harmful.

1. She is clearly passionate about women's liberation and the #MeToo movement. She felt there was an injustice with the proceeding as it related to Kavanaugh. However, there are a few problems with how she chose to convey her disappointment and frustration that demonstrates she has no clue about her White privilege. As a White person, in general, it is never safe to compare one's struggle to another marginalized group.
2. Saying the N-word in any setting, under any circumstances or conditions, is a *no-no*. Just don't do it. It doesn't matter that you see Black folks using the word with each other or in rap lyrics. White people are simply not allowed to say that word, plain and simple. While speaking to a group of people in Illinois in 2017, Ta-Nehisi Coates made it perfectly clear that it is never OK for White people to say the N-word. For, as he eloquently puts it, "[w]ords don't mean anything without context" (Bain 2017). So although a group may choose to use a derogatory term, that does not give other people outside of that community the go-ahead to do so. It is the underlying factor of White privilege that makes White people believe that everything belongs to them and that they are untouchable.

> *When you're White in this country, you're taught that everything belongs to you. You think you have a right to everything ... You're conditioned this way. It's not*

*because your hair is a texture or your skin is light. It's
the fact that the laws and the culture tells you this.
You have a right to go where you want to go, do what
you want to do, be however—and people just got to
accommodate themselves to you.*

—Ta-Nehisi Coates, (Bain 2017)

Furthermore, Coates goes on to say that it is normal for certain cultures or groups of people to use words that others cannot. He gives the example of his wife and her friends calling each other bitches. He knows, and fully understands, that as a man, using that phrase is unacceptable. Instead of feeling like it's unfair or "sexist" that he can't use that term, he comes to a place of acceptance. Being a POC in society often means doing things that others cannot do. So for those who believe it's an "inconvenience" to censor, think of this as the tiniest bit of refraining you can do to show respect.

Using the N-word as the lowest, most horrid possible standard for how White women are being disregarded—as bad as Black people—subconsciously pleads for the world to not treat White women like they treat Black people. Her statement of how terrible society treats and views Black people demonstrates awareness, like in Jane Elliot's experiment. But at the same time, she continued to be inactive in standing up against racism until she saw it spill over to White women. Then and only then did she make the connection. Her delivery was awful, but it gave insight into the way that she and many others will ignore how POCs are treated because it is not their problem.

3. Finally, Bette should not self-proclaim allyship under any circumstances. She is a great singer, actress, maybe even advocate for women's rights, but her allyship is questionable given her statement and reaction after she was called out on her tweet.

CALL TO ACTION

- Process why Bette Midler's tweet was problematic, if not offensive, to communities of color. Can you identify why her allyship is questionable?
- Connect with a person of color and have a discussion about the N-word and its use by White people. Discuss who and under what circumstances a White person can proclaim their allyship.

The issue that keeps arising is that White people don't know how to have courageous, compassionate, and constructive conversations about race while taking the perspective of a person of color. And although literature addressing "White tears," allyship, and White privilege has increased, the majority of these authors are White individuals themselves. Yes, they acknowledge and empower their White counterparts to check each other when defenses begin to rise, exactly what this book is advocating for. However, the question remains: Can one White person accurately teach another White person to be an ally? Open dialogue about race requires listening and engagement, not White fragility, which often encompasses a justification of certain behaviors or shutting down racially charged conversations. I have personally observed the discomfort in White faces when Black people become transparent, real, and raw about how complicit even the most well-intended White person can be and how racism spills over.

White fragility leads to uncomfortable feelings and racial stress for most White folks, giving them a small taste of the daily life of a POC. As one author put it, "[r]acial stress is the result of an interruption of what is racially familiar" (DiAngelo 2011, 103). I believe that for those who initially want to become anti-racist they stumble as to how to respond constructively. They lack effective skills that would allow for productive engagement in courageous conversations. Because there are no clear road maps to allyship and as it is the nature of White people, they will take matters into their own hands. The purpose of this book is to give White folks a road map. There is no guessing needed, as there is a step-by-step guide to allyship that I cover in Part III.

Bette Midler had an opportunity to make it right, to truly show her allyship and where she stands. Instead, she tried to justify rather than own her tweet, overcompensate rather than apologize for her statement, quickly take down her tweet rather than educate other White folks on what allyship really entails, and, last, assume the victim role rather than seizing the opportunity to become a fearless advocate. Be prepared to take the feedback, engage in the conversation, move past the failure, and learn to do it better next time. The lesson is in accepting that privileges are given to you, not earned by you; they happened to you, and they come with responsibility and opportunity.

CHAPTER 6

WHITE GUILT/WHITE SAVIOR

L et's do a check-in. Thank you for acknowledging your White privilege. But please do not move into feeling guilty or wanting to save the world. Stay present.

WHITE GUILT: I DON'T SAY WHAT I MEAN AND I DON'T MEAN WHAT I SAY

Guilt is an emotion and the inner recognition that occurs after an individual does something wrong. It is a natural response to recognizing that one has behaved in a way that is not acceptable or good. White guilt is a term that became popular during the Obama era. Psychologists define White guilt as the dejection White people feel when they witness discriminatory or racist acts (Steele 1990). It occurs when an individual begins to feel guilty for the racist treatment of people of color (POCs) historically and in present times. This collective guilt is also felt when White people are aware of their inability or hesitancy to take action as racial discrimination is happening. While the sting of White guilt occurs after the acknowledgment of White privilege, the response to knowing and acknowledging that guilt often varies. One writer explains that there are healthy and unhealthy responses. "Healthy White guilt" leads to change while "unhealthy White guilt" leads to inaction, victimization, and, furthermore, hatred (Iyer, Leach, and Crosby 2003). Notice that unhealthy White guilt is a trauma reaction marked by avoidance and powerlessness, interconnected with the historical underpinnings of White trauma.

Guilt leads to decisions and beliefs that keep White people stagnant from operating as allies. Psychologists have stated that collective guilt is experienced when people categorize themselves within a group that has committed unjustified harm to another group

(Caouette and Taylor 2007). Some feel guilty for not speaking up, not doing more work for justice, and for not being able to change the course of history. Many White people struggle with guilt when they are enlightened with the truth behind racism, the harsh reality of White colonizers, and their dehumanizing treatment of POCs. This information evokes powerful emotions, shame, and discomfort to the point that some resist further education on the impact of racism in society (Tatum 1994).

For those who struggle with this realization because they do not have a mental illness associated with racism, their brains reject the notion of White superiority, thereby oppressing another group strictly by the color of their skin, their hair texture, their religious affiliation, and so on; logically, it just does not make any sense. It is upon this recognition that White guilt and shame begin to settle in. Many White people start to feel guilty by association and ultimately try to cope with their newfound insight by engaging in denial. To justify the actions of their ancestors, White people have to justify and reframe their view about racism and slavery as a tragedy **instead of something that one race has done to another** (Loewen 1995, 12). Unfortunately, this mindset removes accountability and results in avoiding ownership.

The purpose of White guilt is to allow White people to shift from villain to victim and not take personal responsibility for historical and current oppressive and discriminatory practices enacted and enforced by their people. White guilt is a derailer and a distraction. It leaves POCs feeling responsible for having to comfort White people to alleviate their guilt. This is not just utterly unfair; it is also an exercise in White privilege. Through White guilt, White people turn the tables so that POCs have to care for their fragility.

Although many remain stagnant, others are at the point of recognizing their White guilt and figuring out how to move forward in harmony. For many, this emotional emergence does not occur until they fully understand how privileged they are compared to POCs, their own racial identity development, their awareness of personal bias, and an understanding of how they contribute or perpetuate those biases in everyday practice. This newfound awareness often leads to shame and embarrassment because of the belief that others will perceive Whiteness as something negative (Swim and Miller 1999).

WHITE FRAGILITY: AREN'T I THE REAL VICTIM?

Some White people who feel really guilty for something they have done often attempt to make restitution to the victims. Unhealthy responses lead to people focusing solely on their guilt, thereby falling into victimhood, and not what they can do about it. Some are too frail to handle the hard-core truth about their actions. This is also known as "White Fragility." White fragility was coined by Robin DiAngelo, a White ally sociologist. White fragility is the inability to tolerate racial stress which triggers defensive emotions such as anger, fear, and guilt (DiAngelo 2015). In *White Fragility: Why It's So Hard To Talk To White People About Racism*, Dr. DiAngelo goes on to describe, in detail, the defensive nature of White people when they are racially challenged and the resistance it creates to sustaining change. Because White people live in a world where racial issues aren't thoroughly discussed, they are known to protect each other from racial discomfort. Think about it: even the term *White people* may make readers feel uncomfortable because Whites are so used to being "the" people. Instead of being educated and exposing racial misunderstandings, many only take the cultural competency training required of them. In a recent conversation with a nonprofit led by a White woman who wanted me to do an Urban Trauma training, she specifically said during the discovery meeting that we don't have to talk about racism, microaggressions, or implicit bias, that her staff has already been trained on those topics. Got it: so centuries of pain and continued discrimination were summarized in an eight-hour training and the leaders and staff of this nonprofit are golden. I think not.

For this reason, White fragility prevents the work of allyship from being completed because many become silent, withdrawn, and/or shut down, instead of correcting each other when racism, stereotypes, or racial biases occur. White fragility is not speaking up when given an opportunity to advocate and challenge individual instances of racism so as not to disturb the status quo. For example, let's say Rachel and Juan were at a company dinner with their boss, Tom. Tom makes a comment about Juan's heavy accent and how it is distracting in their work environment because people can't understand him. Rachel instantly knows that Tom's statement is a microassault. But instead of correcting him, she remains silent. Despite Rachel and Juan having lots of conversations about race, discriminatory immigration policy, and racism—and Tom's racist and rude remarks to many POCs in the office—she allows her White fragility and the fear of Tom's White fragility to keep her frozen. The moment a White person senses their racial belonging may be shattered if they speak up, they become destabilized (DiAngelo 2018). White privilege and fragility go hand in hand, producing further resistance to progress.

On the other hand, when White fragility is recognized, White privilege goes a long way. For instance, Senator Kirsten Elizabeth Gillibrand, at the August 2018 CNN Democratic presidential primary debate, talked about using White privilege to educate other White people on institutional racism and hold them accountable. She used her platform to explain what privilege is and how she benefits from it. Furthermore, from her own experience, Gillibrand believed that she could be an advocate for racial justice and the fight for equality by appealing to those that look like her. She used her platform to challenge White privilege and expose institutional racism.

The responsibility should not fall on POCs to educate White people on how they are exercising their privilege, using microaggressions, or demonstrating racist tendencies. White allyship and the responsible use of White privilege can be fueled to actively practicing anti-racism. **I want to be clear about this: allyship is not needed because communities of color expect anyone to lead them or save them. Instead, allyship is needed to actively fight and dismantle racist structures built by White people to most certainly benefit White people.**

CALL TO ACTION

The truth about how to properly use your privilege lies in the answer to my next question. Are you willing to give up your comfort, the comfort of being acceptable to other White people, to practice anti-racism in all aspects of your life?

- List three areas in which you're willing to step away from your privilege and comfort in service to racial justice right now. They don't have to be heroic or huge, just a step farther along the path.
- What moves or inspires you to do this work? Make a mission statement for yourself that you can look back on when the process feels difficult. Your desire for this outcome has to be stronger than the resistance, both internal and external. Fuel that motivation.
- When you are at the end of your life, how do you want to be remembered? Jot down some notes. What would you want people to say about your contributions to humanity?

WHITE SAVIOR: I AM NOT RACIST

Historically, a White savior is someone who comes in to "save" those less fortunate than them. It is the misguided desire to help with the mind-set that you, a White person, knows what the marginalized community needs better than the community does (Fisher 2017). White savior industrial complex was coined in 2012 by Nigerian American novelist Teju Cole. It occurs when people are rewarded for "saving" those less fortunate than themselves. Although perhaps well intended, it is ultimately a misguided desire to help people who appear impoverished or less than, not equal to (Fisher 2016). The only reason White saviorism has a platform is because of the policies that White people have created that helped maintain the system of oppression, poverty, and corruption (Aronson 2017). It is often seen as self-serving in the eyes of those who are less fortunate. The solution is simple: communities of color do not need a White savior. We just need White people to stop creating systems geared toward destroying us. Philanthropic institutions are a relevant example.

The desire to be, and to be known as, a good White person stems from the recognition that Whiteness can be perceived as problematic, a recognition that White people try to escape from by being demonstrably different from that perception. Giving to charitable causes is one of the easiest ways to enact saviorhood. In *Decolonizing Wealth: Indigenous Wisdom to Heal Divides and Restore Balance*, author Edgar Villanueva (2018), of the Lumbee Tribe in North Carolina, makes mention of how the word *philanthropy* has been tossed around and abused. Philanthropy is not an act of doing but an act of being. However, for those who are privileged, entitled, and fortunate, this type of self-sacrifice is a stretch. Villanueva describes this as an altruistic mindset. It remains in the framework of the "us versus them" mentality. Philanthropy is meant to be a reciprocal relationship. It's not about dollars but about showing up and making an impact on society without expecting a reward or even acknowledgment. Instead, what happens in real life is that for many POC nonprofit leaders, they continue to experience isolation, power struggles with White grant-makers, and a great deal of hardship in their efforts to help their community. They lose out on receiving grants to their White counterparts and often have to fight for funding support with other White nonprofits, many of which have grant writers and staff that grassroots POC-led organizations cannot afford because they lack general operating support. In addition, even when White-led nonprofits receive funding and are working with a majority diverse community, they do not create a POC supply chain to do business with or contract with, or support the work of POC-led nonprofits.

Villanueva (2018) suggests that for many White people working in philanthropy, their main focus is to continue preserving wealth through what is called "colonial-style" exploitation of resources, cheap labor, and tax evasion. Those who are stuck in the "White savior" mentality hoard this wealth and use it to dominate and control the seekers and recipients of those funds. Nonprofits led by White leaders benefit from appearing to care for diverse communities and instead exploit them for their benefit. They have connections to donors and are in control of the narrative; they create photo ops with marginalized Black or Brown kids seeking to create a look-good, feel-good picture rather than streaming the money down to those who need it the most. This stolen money, as Villanueva describes it, is used as a source of control and power. In fact, a 2017 research conducted by Charity Commissions found that 92 percent of foundation executive directors were White (Derosier 2020).

Most important, the very people that philanthropies are supposed to help are heavily scrutinized while not given any assistance or support through that process (e.g., grassroots organizations, POC-led organizations, nonprofits, etc.). Villanueva (2018, 2) says it best: "Money is my medicine, and in order to heal what hurts, to come back together as one human race, and to restore balance to the land, we need to decolonize wealth." He highlights Native wisdom by underscoring this very basic principle. "You don't choose the medicine—the medicine chooses you" (Villanueva 2018). I often wonder if the interest yielded from the accumulated wealth portfolios of all foundations whose primary mission is to provide grant-making to the underserved were used as a reparation strategy, how much healing and stabilization could occur in communities of color?

Another way to be known as a good White person is by being surrounded by Black or Brown people, adopting children of other races, or being in an interracial relationship. If, as a reader, you identify with one of these categories, examine if these relationships act as a pardon from the responsibility of your Whiteness or are they truly aligned to the deepest level of love and often self-sacrifice needed to protect the Black and Brown people you are in a relationship with and, by default, their community. Are these relationships an attempt to invalidate charges of racism or privilege by proving that one has always been connected to POCs and "get them"? Is it an attempt to demonstrate friendship and solidarity with POCs who have been oppressed? To make up for the errors of your ancestors, seeking reassurance, acceptance, and absolution?

An authentic conversation and personal evaluation are required here. Friendships, relationships, and closeness to POCs do not exempt people from their privilege. In a society where "White" is ideal, one can use so-called Black friendships to leverage their standing within, and between, the marginalized community and subconsciously feel superior (DiAngelo 2015). Too many times, White people have used common sayings to "prove" they're not racist and exemplify themselves. "I have Black friends," "I don't see color," "My son is married to an Asian woman," and so on and so on. It's a misconception that proximity to melanin immunizes White people from doing or saying racist things. What many don't know is that the "Black friend" as a buffer was a tactic used by slave owners to portray a false narrative that they were beloved by the enslaved they subjugated.

Slave owners were good at manipulating slaves to maintain power, privilege, and superiority over them. They would go so far as to treat those who served in the house, who were usually light-skinned, with more respect than those out on the field—the emergence of colorism in the Black community. Some slave owners even formed significant, often forced, relationships with the enslaved, which often included raping women and having mixed children. Mixed children were then treated with "special" favor. This favoritism not only caused a divide within the enslaved; it also created a loyalty between master and those "highly esteemed" slaves. This was a tactic used to keep enslaved people content, comfortable, and convince them to "keep up the good work" (Fortner 2008). It was the slave owners who befriended the enslaved, and, at times, treated those they owned as if they were family so the slave owner would be deemed a good master. This mentality gave some more savage slave owners justification as to why they were different from other slave owners; they were more like friends. However, being popular amongst the enslaved did not mean that slave owners were doing what was best for those they enslaved. It was strictly about manipulation and mind control.

White saviors tend to make assumptions about the best way to come in and save the day. It is the thought that one is becoming a trusted ally. Saviorism is an emotionally rewarding feeling. Saviors feel that they made a contribution to a worthy cause, and in turn, the "making a difference" box is checked. In reality, it is self-serving, not helpful, and a waste of time. White saviors do not know how to use their privilege for racial equality or to gain equity largely because they go about it the wrong way. How does this manifest? Think of the White suburban teacher working in an urban school district trying to save students of color and educate them the right way, a "messianic" White savior, rescuing poor little Black and Brown kids from a sad fate. Whether it's to make up for their guilt or an act of redemption, the White savior complex often leads to more issues than solving them.

My challenge with White saviors is that their friendship circle, urban career options, missions, and/or their philanthropic giving come with limitations. Most White saviors whom I have encountered are reluctant to engage in blunt conversations about race. During a training session at a predominately affluent school district a few years ago, a White teacher stood up in an audience of more than 100 educators and yelled at me, abruptly interrupting my talk, stating that I was calling him a racist. He proclaimed with vigor that he was not a racist because he donates clothes to the immigrant Latinx families who were "invading" his predominantly White school district. Huh? This level of defensiveness highlights that this teacher had not done the necessary work to become a true ally; instead, his comment presents itself as a general failure to acknowledge his fear of racial migration and how that would shift the culture in their elite White school and community. Hiding behind the cloak of saviorism, White saviors are usually insecure, lack identity formation, and approach racial equity with arrogance, ignorance, and, ultimately, cause harm. Those who are uncomfortable talking about race or get defensive against conversation focused on racism are the worst offenders, warming the bench just waiting for the opportunity to play savior all the while standing by as one vulnerable community after another is destroyed.

Side note: as a POC who provides training all the time on this topic, I have been disrespected more times than I can count. I often wonder: If I were a White male speaking on this same topic, would White audience members feel emboldened to behave in this same manner?

Let's now focus on the White teacher who has chosen to teach in an urban school district and sees him- or herself as an ally. There are many young White teachers who complete their degrees and start their careers teaching in urban school districts. There are programs that provide a platform and structure for teachers to begin their professional journey in the inner city, whose student populations are composed mostly of Black and Brown low-income kids, and, in turn, these teachers receive loan repayment or some type of incentive. I believe that many White teachers are supporters of social justice (more on this term in Part III). The beginning of the school year is typically full of promise, and the possibility of changing lives is imminent.

There are three types of White teachers who decide to teach in urban settings:

Type 1: **The delightfully confused.** They do not have enough teaching experience to teach in a more affluent town, sometimes the town that they live in. As a result, they must put in a few years in an urban setting until they can gain enough experience and find employment in a more desirable district. Or they are seeking loan forgiveness. Both are external factors for their decision to teach in an urban environment that have little to do with their desire to do so.

Type 2: **The White savior.** This is the teacher who, to some extent, understands their privilege but has not done the work to become an ally. This teacher stays in the urban school district every year, becoming more and more disappointed and disillusioned because their teaching methods are not effective as well as because their lofty expectation of saving kids does not really work. At times, their savior complex turns into apathy, and they begin to resent being overworked and underpaid, having to buy their own materials for their classrooms. This type of teacher begins to target Black boys who are often the most difficult for them to engage with and/or who act out in their classrooms. The general worldview of this White teacher is that he/she always gets the "bad" Black and Brown kids. They blame the children, the school system, and the families for their failure to educate and create a positive learning environment. In an effort to carry forward their victimhood, they engage in precipitous profiling, whereby Black and Brown boys are "looked at" and rerouted before classroom assignments are determined.

Type 3:   **The ally.** This White teacher is rare, but they exist. This teacher is not only aware of their privilege but believes fundamentally in building a relationship with each and every child and parent. Although they may not understand the process of becoming an ally, they do understand the importance of relationships, in general, and in Black and Brown communities, in particular. This is the teacher who selects the girl or boy who is struggling academically or behaviorally to be their helper, who stays after school, who engages the parents without judgment, even those who do not show up to parent/teacher night. Most importantly, this teacher-ally remains flexible and opens a space where parents who are concerned, and sometimes carry shame, can talk about their kids. This teacher-ally becomes a co-parent with the family, teaching about Black, Latinx, and Indigenous history just as much as they teach about White history or the Holocaust. This teacher-ally seeks out support from her diverse colleagues, taking advice on how to deal with attachment problems, trauma, and even introverts. This teacher-ally changes lives not because she wants to be anybody's savior but because she understands that she chose this profession, she chose this job, and she needs to show up to the job fit for duty. This positive reinforcement is so important that CNN (LaMotte 2020) reported that teachers who praise their students instead of punishing them saw a 30 percent increase in good behavior and academic achievement. Those teachers who don't pinpoint negative behavior or make Black and Brown students feel like criminals are the ones that really make a difference.

Owning your own choices is critical in the path to allyship. The reality is that all children, despite their race, want to learn. They want to be reinforced. They want to succeed. I have never heard a child, in all my years as a psychologist, say that they want to fail. It is the job of teachers to teach. No one said it was going to be easy. If a teacher's true passion is to educate in an urban environment, then as a teacher, you are a parent, a therapist, a coach, a healer, and so much more.

CALL TO ACTION FOR TEACHERS

If you are a White teacher who is interested in becoming an ally, read this section carefully:

Step 1: Understand that you choose to educate Black and Brown kids in an urban school district.

Step 2: Recognize that at times you stand in front of your classroom feeling lost, hopeless, and stuck. You

---

wonder to yourself, "Why am I here? I want to go somewhere else," or "These kids don't want to learn, they behave terribly; they don't care about school and whether they pass or fail." These are normal feelings, but you don't have to act on them.

Step 3: Build relationships with your most difficult students and parents. Challenge your belief system and ground it on the principle that every kid wants to succeed and every parent wants to be a good parent. I know it is hard to believe this when you sit in a parent/teacher conference and only one or two parents show up, and in your subconscious, it is confirmation that Black and Brown parents do not care about their children. Challenge this negative worldview and humanize them, show compassion, be flexible, and, most important, show that you are equally invested in their success.

During the time that my daughter was in public school, she encountered all three of these White teacher types. My daughter is a bright 15-year old #Blackgirlmagic who claims, because of her middle-class upbringing, to be "privileged, yet not entitled." As I stated previously, as a toddler, we taught her how to code-switch between Black and White environments, after having a run-in with a Type 1 preschool teacher. Our daughter has code-switching down to a science. Between her code-switching skills and the supplementary racial socialization, plus pan-African teachings we do at home to reinforce her racial identity and self-esteem, she is solid in who she is and what she represents. She does not allow what a teacher thinks of her to define who she is; she creates the definition and the teachers follow suit. Now, we did this intentionally because we knew what we were up against. But, despite all the support we provided her, there were moments when we had to show up to that school and deal with a Type 1 teacher who did not do their homework about our daughter and her parents.

Once the rules of engagement were established and we course-corrected, that school year usually went very well. I saw the difference in how she was treated (different, special) versus the other Black and Brown students in the classroom. She would come home with stories about so-and-so who acted out in class and the teacher's reaction to that child. As representatives, we felt responsible for the village. My husband spent time in the classroom engaging some of the boys; I offered support, went on school trips, joined the parent/teacher organization, volunteered, and became an active member of the school community. Now I believe all parents should do this, but I did it because I needed to keep a watchful eye on my child and other people's children too.

I share this story for two reasons: first, to demonstrate to White teachers the level of effort that it takes parents of color to ensure academic success for their child in public schools and, second, to show the shift in responsibility when the teacher is not an ally. It moves from a collaborative partnership to an adversarial one. We are no longer a team; you are both my child's teacher and her enemy. No matter the Type 1, 2, or 3, I know that for the majority of White teachers, this is not the environment they want to create. My final recommendation: align your intentions with your behaviors and how you show up in the classroom.

I could not end this section before supporting Type 2 teachers to move into teacher-ally, Type 3. So this call to action is for you. Recognize and embrace the sense of guilt and shame for what your White ancestors have done and your desire to make amends. If you feel guilty for not speaking up, for not doing more work for justice, and for being unable to change the course of history, remember that tomorrow still exists, that you can do it differently. Learn from your mistakes; go to a training session on urban education taught by POCs; connect with diverse teachers who are succeeding in their classrooms (not those who are apathetic). Do not remain stagnant. At the point of recognizing your White guilt, choose to be an ally, not a savior. Recognize that this emotional emergence does not occur until you fully understand how privileged you are compared to POCs and you gain an awareness of your personal bias. Change yourself and I promise that you will impact countless numbers of kids in your lifetime. You got this!

STORY

Lisa Votto, Licensed Family and Marriage Therapist
White woman working in social services,
adoptive parent of a Brown child

I am a White, middle-aged heterosexual female. Allyship has been a lifelong process for me, starting far back into childhood and continuing today. Recently I took an implicit bias test and was shocked at what I learned, forcing me to look more closely at my own privilege and the ally identity I've held for years.

From a young age, I saw myself as a person who had an eye for injustice. Growing up in a lower-middle-class neighborhood consisting mostly of Italian American families like mine, diversity was not commonplace. When a Black family moved into our neighborhood, there were whispers and slurs behind their backs. I was angered by the behavior of "my" people then. I made it a point to reach out and become friendly with the new family, with the full support of my mother and father.

I was the daughter who asked her parents to take me to bring some toys to a toddler I often passed riding on the bus with my mom; she played with just an old pot on her porch. I was the kid who got the sense beat into me at age 12 by older teens who were bullying my friend in a wheelchair and I demanded that they stop. I was the teen who didn't speak to my grandfather for years after he used a racial slur in the presence of my Black friend; we weren't speaking when he died. When I was pulled over by police in my 20s and the officer told me he thought I was a "spic" then let me go, I filed a complaint. I wanted there to be justice in the world. Anything less felt wrong to me.

As I grew into adulthood, my views, along with my social circle, expanded. I developed and maintained a close group of friends, consisting of many POCs. I continued to be angered by racism. When Trayvon Martin was murdered, I initiated conversations with my Black and Brown teenage nephews and godsons about racism, about being safe when (not *if*) encountered by police. I talked to them about how the world would see them as they grew into adult Black men and then urged them to seek other positive Brown and Black men and women to learn from.

I moved forward in a career in social work and remained committed to matters of social justice. Working with at-risk youth in my community only reinforced the many injustices I had seen in the news: the school-to-prison pipeline, a lack of quality services for Black/Brown youth, and unfair legal processes, just to name only a few. I vocalized these concerns at every turn to whoever had the power. I advocated for the youth I worked with, advocated so that they would receive even a fraction of the justice they deserved. I was the social worker who fought for the arrest of a White woman who sexually assaulted a 15-year-old Black boy. "No," I told the detective, "they were *not* dating, and we wouldn't be having this conversation if the races were reversed." I was the one who asked a warden at a prison why the mental health unit in corrections consisted of all White inmates while the "behavior" unit was filled with Black and Brown young men. I asked a judge to provide me with the percentage of court-ordered psychological evaluations done on Black and Brown youth with the frequency of conduct disorder diagnosis versus other mental health disorders related to trauma. I asked and I asked and I asked. I kept bringing up the conversations despite the disdain I received, despite the names I was called, despite the adverse effects it had on my career. I recognized then as I recognize now that I had a responsibility to speak out in a way that POCs are not able to.

I learned that I was able to deliver messages that wouldn't get delivered otherwise and that there was power in this. In most cases, the person I confronted would take a moment, appearing unsettled and taken aback at being called out. They would reply with something that was most often deflective. Each and every time, my question or comment would go unanswered. The satisfaction I got was that I was able to convey to them "I see you, I see what's happening here, and I'm exposing it."

My adopted daughter is Afro-Caribbean. Her biological roots run through Africa to the Dominican Republic to Puerto Rico and to slavery in the Deep South of United States. Her chocolate skin and curly hair are much different from mine. Some people smile at us, asking questions as if it's their place to understand how I am her mother; others sneer, imagining where she came from. I am keenly aware of how the world will see her as she matures into an intelligent, confident, and strong Black woman. The awareness fills me with an uneasy combination of pride and fear—pride because with the help of my village, she will always know who she is and where she came from and fear because who she represents is what some feel needs to be stifled and extinguished in our country. My daughter is the spirit of her ancestors and the spirit of how I am raising her now. There is a fire inside her, a fire that combines all this richness deep within, propelling her to be extraordinary.

And I continue to fight. I fight so that her public school in our heavily immigrant-populated community gets a playground, just like all the other schools in different neighborhoods, just blocks away. I fight so that her ballet instructors recognize her hair care needs are different from the blonde-haired girls. I fight so that flesh-colored and beige are *not* synonymous. I know that police do indeed murder unarmed Black and Brown civilians at a higher rate than White ones. I admit that getting pulled over by the police is *never* a life and death situation for me. *Never.* I have to admit that a mere traffic stop can kill one of my loved ones. I have an obligation to admit my White privilege is real. It doesn't mean I want it, it doesn't mean it's not ugly, but it is *real.* I call out my people when they need to be called out. I support my Black and Brown brothers and sisters fighting the good fight, and I do so publicly.

I've also learned what *not* to do. I no longer try to compare my meager experiences of injustices with those faced by POCs. Privilege is inherent to being a White woman. I stopped talking so much and started listening more. I ask questions. I never use the N-word. Ever. I know this word is off-limits to White people in any context, under any circumstances.

You can't sign up for a class and learn how to be an ally. Allyship lives inside you. It's a commitment. It's a clear sense of right and wrong. It's a hunger for justice. It's about humility. It's listening instead of talking. It's about losing friends. Allyship carries with it a duty to speak out, a duty to act on all those feelings and beliefs. It is a belief and acceptance that White privilege is not a myth, that there's no such thing as reverse racism. Allyship is being just as willing to say these things in a room filled with Black and Brown people as you are with saying these things in a room filled with White people. Allyship is using privilege to move people to change.

Allyship changes you. It changes your circle of friends. Your allyship will expose the racism of others in your life: friends, family members, coworkers. Allyship complicates your relationships; it can be isolating. I have learned things about loved ones I would have never known if I didn't speak my truth and share my feelings. I made conscious decisions to cut people out of my life based on my beliefs, and some have cut me out. Allyship is not easy.

Conversely, I have also benefited by connecting with like-minded people. I've been honored to be invited into the inner circles of POCs, embraced as an ally and trusted with learning more about their feelings and struggles. Allyship is a blessing and an honor.

Allyship also means getting frustrated and angry because progress takes so long and my people can't get their shit together. But I keep asking questions. And I listen. And I speak up. And I speak out. And I will do this all the days of my life, as it began when I was a child and continues as I raise my own child in this world filled with injustices and hate. Somewhere buried within, I choose to believe there is hope, there is equity, and there is peace. Perhaps that's just my privilege speaking.

Back to my results from the Harvard University Project Implicit Association Test (https://implicit.harvard.edu/implicit/takeatest.html). I was eager to see a stellar outcome, validating my own identity as an ally. To my dismay, I learned that my testing indicates I moderately favor White over Black. Not mildly, not somewhat, but *moderately*. I moderately favor White over Black. It was easier for me to associate White with good and Black with bad. As this sunk in, I found myself feeling beyond disappointed. I have a significant bias! I never considered the results of this test would be anything other than a further demonstration of my allyship and my lens of equality. But no.

What does this mean for me? Am I an imposter? Should I no longer be allowed to identify myself as an ally? How does this affect my ability to effectively parent my child, a child of color? And the ultimate question, What can I do to reverse this result?

I immediately called Dr. Akbar to share my disgrace and confusion. Of course, she wasn't surprised, nor was she horrified. She asked me to dig even deeper, to accept my biases as I have done in the past to recognize and integrate my White privilege.

What does my result mean on a larger scale? It means that even for a person who is aware, insightful, and committed to racial justice, the internal messages society has ingrained in me are undeniable. These messages are stronger than our intent as individuals. If someone, like me, with a strong commitment to racial justice since childhood can score as moderately biased, then there's no doubt that the vast majority of people in society are highly biased! So it's more common than not to have a significant level of implicit bias.

This is the reality of the society in which we live. No, I'm not an imposter. What I will do is share this result with others in conversations about racial justice and invite others to take the test and use the results to consider how this impacts our interaction with POCs. The presence of bias is undeniable. I choose to accept the results and use them to further advance my personal growth and insight and to spread this awareness to others. I look to the future, with the hope that one day, implicit bias will *not* be the norm.

CHAPTER 7

UNPACKING WHITE WOMEN AS ALLIES

ARE WHITE WOMEN COMPLICIT?

"Hell hath no fury like a White woman crying" (Accapadi 2007). It is said that White women's tears are often weapons of mass destruction (Ajai 2017). In light of their oppression, abuse, and subjugation under the hands of White men, some White women have taken full advantage of their privilege by assuming a position of oppressor or victim. During the times of slavery, White women were complicit in the abuse and terror inflicted on slaves as the wives of slave owners. At times, the worst assaults against Black and Brown bodies were incited by White women.

In the movie *The BlacKkKlansman* (Lee 2018), which took place in the 1970s, there was a scene during which the wife of a KKK member not just supported the KKK cause but also assisted in some of the planning and execution of the group's diabolical actions. During a deep conversation with colleagues of color debriefing the movie and its message, a realization set in during the discussion: every Klansman has a White mother. What happened during the upbringing of these White boys who eventually became White men that allowed them to turn into rapists, abusers, and murderers of people of color (POCs)? Undoubtedly, many of these women believe that they were instilling morals and values in their sons. Many went to church and felt they were "good" mothers and "good" women.

In another movie *Harriet* (Lemmons 2019), about Harriet Tubman, the White wife of a slave owner also promoted hatred against slaves on the plantation, even after the husband died. Although there was an opportunity for her to do something different as the head of the plantation, she continued the practice of enslavement, with her son taking charge where his father left off. She could have changed the legacy of her family through her son, redirecting his behavior by uprooting his hatred toward the enslaved

Black people on their plantation. Examining various movies about enslavement brought about one sad and resounding conclusion: directors and producers have accurately depicted all White female characters in a similar way. And sadly, most of these scripts are based on factual historical findings.

THE WRONGFULLY ACCUSED

The tragic case of Emmett Till illustrates yet another instance of a White woman wrongfully accusing a 14-year-old boy of raping her in 1955. This accusation led to a mob of White men brutally beating him to death, committing murder without an ounce of justice. It wasn't until 2018 that the victim recanted her accusation, and with White tears, she reported that she fabricated the story.

In the 1980s, another White woman punished and persecuted five innocent boys, ages 14 to 16, in the case of the Central Park Five. The lives of these men were destroyed by a structurally racist system, used as leverage by a White attorney who relentlessly targeted these Black and Brown boys, built a false case against them, and did not stop until she obtained a conviction. This same White attorney was comfortably teaching at Columbia University until Ava DuVernay's (2019) Netflix series *When They See Us* outed her and the community began to demand her removal but only after she made millions selling novels.

Did the system fail these boys, or are the stewards of these structures, many of whom are racist, able to manipulate the system so POCs are stuck in a cycle of oppression? White women continue using the same playbook, voting against their own best interest for the sake of unity with White men, calling the police on Black people (#BBQBecky, Karens) for no reason, all for the sake of weaponizing Blackness.

These incidents demonstrate the power and privilege White women can render to manipulate and dominate POCs (Hamad 2019). If a White woman is challenged or uncomfortable with something a POC says, all she has to do is shed alligator tears before she is comforted and pacified. White men will degrade White women, who in turn do the same to POCs, and simultaneously, these same White women will align with White men despite the harm they are causing them or others. This is called the cycle of abuse by psychologists.

White women have benefited greatly as the "mothers of slavery." What is clear throughout the ages is that there are White women allies who demonstrate a questionable approach to supporting POC causes, and this phenomenon has been a constant battle since the women's rights movement.

VOTING RIGHTS

The most historic example of allyship would be the role Black women took during the women's suffrage movement in 1913. Before the march, women suffragists gathered in Seneca Falls, New York, in July 1848, to advocate for the rights of White women to vote. The participants were middle- and upper-class White women, a cadre of White men supporters, and one African American male, Frederick Douglass. No Black women were invited. Over time, it was clear that Black women were needed as an integral part of the women's rights movement and that voting rights were not just reserved for White women but for Black women and all women as well.

Trying to work together taught Black women and White women about the power of interracial connection and shed light on some deep dissimilarities. Both groups of women desired voting rights but for different reasons. White women were seeking the vote as a symbol of parity with their husbands and brothers. Black women were seeking the ballot for them, Black men, and as a means of empowering the Black community.

As the fight for women's rights heated up, so did the tension between Black and White women. Research shows that Black women's suffrage clubs that wanted to align with the national White suffrage movement were discouraged from doing so on the grounds that admitting them might anger White southerners (Staples 2018). In May 1851, African American abolitionist Sojourner Truth spoke at a women's rights convention in Akron, Ohio. The convention organizers, Frances Dana Gage and other White feminists, depicted Truth as an ally to White audiences, and as genuine allies, together they would fight for all women's rights. However, their voices were controlled and White suffragists were not open to inclusion, in spite of the sheer advantage of all women—Black, White, Native, immigrants—uniting.

It wasn't until the 20th century and the rise of Black suffragist leaders that White women were challenged to reflect on the compounding oppressions and systemic violence that Black women endured during enslavement. Black legal scholar Kimberle Crenshaw (1989, 149) gives this analogy: "Discrimination, like traffic through an intersection, may flow in one direction, and it may flow in another. If an accident happens in an intersection, it can be caused by cars traveling from any number of directions and, sometimes, from all of them." It shows that whereas White women have traditionally been treated as delicate and subordinate to White men, Black women have been denigrated and subject to the racist abuse that is a foundational element of U.S. society.

Although most faces associated with White supremacy have been White men, that does not mean that White women haven't participated. Nowadays, White women often enter the nonprofit world thinking that they can stand in the gap for POCs, but their biases and White supremacy surface. In her article "White Women

Doing White Supremacy in Nonprofit Culture," Heather Laine Talley (2019) talks about how nonprofits led by non-POCs say that they want to be multicultural but that in reality, those other cultures have to adapt and conform to the already established White cultural norms.

NOT-FOR-PROFIT

As a POC who works in the intersection of psychology and racial justice, I often find myself in a room full of well-intended White people who, with passion, have decided to focus their professional career on charitable work, mostly in the nonprofit space. White women occupy most of the executive positions in nonprofits across the country, upward of 87 percent (Battalia Winston 2017).

I have witnessed supportive White women in positions of power who simply do not help other POC leaders. They claim with words that they are in the fight for racial justice, yet in deed, their staff do not reflect the population they serve, they do not seem to uplift or advance other grassroots or minority-led organizers that are making an impact, and they tend to hoard as much of the funding as possible, keeping POCs out or fighting for the crumbs that are left behind. On the occasion that there are leaders of color in the organization, they often feel stifled and suffocated, knowing that the top leadership feels intimidated or simply does not want to share their power. Although I have a general distrust of White intention (this is historical, generational, and currently heavy in our political climate, so it's nothing personal), I would be foolish to believe that we alone can fight for social and racial justice.

Actor, writer, and producer Issa Rae does a phenomenal job of illustrating this conflict throughout her HBO special *Insecure* (Matsoukas et al. 2016–). In the show, Rae works at a nonprofit known as "We Got Ya'll." The show illustrates that POCs who work in nonprofits, among the mostly White upper-class millennials, experience a great deal of race-based distress. Rae's boss, a White woman, repeatedly says she wants to "save the children from the 'hood." However, her methods are stereotypical and covertly racist. For instance, the name of her organization alone is bothersome. "We Got Ya'll": Do White people really have us? Then the original logo she designed illustrated three Black kids being cradled in a pair of White hands, which perpetuates White saviorism. The character of the White nonprofit leader continued to give the idea that POC youth need constant saving, especially by White people. In fact, many of Issa's coworkers are dealing with their own biases and seek to have their savior complex fulfilled while working with Black and Latinx youth. They believe that youth become disengaged from the program due to drugs, gang involvement, and pregnancy rather than problems the nonprofit workers themselves are causing in failing to connect. Young POCs have a keen sense of picking up on authenticity and intention. Saviorism of this kind destroys trust and builds resistance to program interest.

Rae's character finally decides to quit her job with no real future employment plan because she is unable to deal with the incongruent feeling of selling out as well as the daily power-packed combo of White woman microaggressive behavior and White saviorism.

Many times, when White leadership hires a POC, it becomes the POC's job to "make a difference" and highlight diversity issues. In reality, those POCs begin to notice harmful workplace norms that typically go under the radar. When they begin to point out the flaws and inequities at work, the White leadership become easily offended and narrow-minded. POCs, especially women, are often dismissed or ignored when they speak up about racism. There is a huge amount of denial. Some are told that decisions are based on data and not emotion. There is an unwillingness within White-led companies to hear or believe their marginalized employees.

Oftentimes, the racism White women perpetuate is less visible; it is more covert and passive-aggressive. Passive-aggressive feedback shows up as indirect communication or downright lying. White women use these communication styles to avoid confrontation about their White privilege and conflict about their underlying bias and racist ideology (Talley 2019). White women struggle with acknowledging their power. Many White women do not claim their power publicly, but they will passively continue to take the lead on projects, take the promotion meant for the diversity hire, negotiate and secure higher salaries than men and women of color, and, at times, "inadvertently" exclude ethnic diversity representation from their teams.

Then there are those White women who want to show up as the "best ally in the room" and often try to do so by publicly distinguishing themselves from other White women and men and attempting to build relationships with POCs. But when the important moments arrive, when those women are called on to stand up against a racist company decision or to give something up that would show actual allyship, they are nowhere to be seen.

My work revolves around helping the underserved. For the majority of my career, I have worked in community health and with nonprofit agencies. However, I am usually not invited to meetings around policymaking, grant opportunities, collaborative workgroups, or new mental health initiatives in my state. But on the rare occasion that I am, I am one of the few women of color in the room. I am an expert in Urban Trauma. I created the Urban Trauma framework from decades of personal experience, education, and research. I took years to curate this carefully thought-out concept for professionals in my field to use as a tool of communication regarding the complexity of race-based trauma. Yet, in spite of my expertise, my Ivy League background, and my passion for the work, there are many who will not invite me to lead or support critical discussions/decisions that will impact my community.

When White women acknowledge their privilege and see these dynamics, real opportunities for allyship open up. I remember speaking to my publisher, a lesbian White woman, when we were getting ready to release my first book, *Urban Trauma: A Legacy of Racism* (Akbar 2017): I wanted to know how to protect and copyright my framework. Like many POCs who innovate, we have seen historically how our ideas and concepts have been appropriated by White people, so my concern was based on historical fact. I had been thinking about this for some time but never quite knew how to bring it up during our publishing calls. I feared she would think I was paranoid and dismiss my concerns, leaving me feeling invalidated and professionally vulnerable. Because we were still developing trust and I was gauging her level of allyship, I felt conflicted about bringing up the topic of protecting my work from, well, White people, her people.

During one of our weekly video calls, I decided to broach the subject. With vulnerability, I said, "Jenn, I have something very serious I need to ask you." I went on to explain that I have seen colleagues' work and ideas taken, with no recognition or regard for their contribution to the body of work or the innovation around their programs. Although Jenn did not dismiss my concern, I perceived that she was not as worried as I was about this matter. I also softened my delivery because I did not want to single out White women and make her feel bad.

Finally, I said to her in a direct manner, "I need you to think like a White person, not an ally. What would you do if you came across my work and it was not protected in any meaningful way? Seriously, Jenn, please think White." There was a moment of silence, perhaps due to shock, or maybe because of the agony in my voice, a tone of desperation.

I could see her observable discomfort, but she took a deep breath and bravely plowed through the conversation. "Well, if I were to think like a White person, I would take your concept, use it to

benefit my work and organization, not acknowledge your author-
ship, and discredit any claims that this was solely yours to use."

OK, I thought, now we are getting somewhere. I replied, "Great,
so given that, how would I protect it?"

With a chuckle, she responded, "That is simple: a trademark."

I stared at her through the screen for a moment and said,
"A what?"

She laughed with me. "Let's get this baby up to an attorney so
we can copyright and obtain a federal trademark for Urban Trauma.
This will give you quite a bit of protection." For the first time in a
while, I felt the warmth of allyship.

This ally's advice changed the way I disseminated my work to
the world. I had to learn the White way so that I could get it right.

Side note: this doesn't always work out, but sometimes it does.
I wish I could say that trademarking my work eliminated importers
who were trying to steal. It, unfortunately, did not. In fact, a local
organization run mostly by White women tried to book me for a
training event months after the release of my book, but they did not
want to pay my fee. Several months later, we got a call from another
organization, headed by a White woman, who wanted to provide
training for her staff on Urban Trauma. She said that as a nonprofit,
they did not have training dollars and asked if I would be willing
to do the training pro bono. We told her that I was unable to work
for free at that time, but that we would keep her posted if anything
changed. She then informed my team that she would buy a ticket for
the talk I was doing a few weeks later. My staff was shocked since all
the events that were in the pipeline were closed to the public.

Later on, we discovered that the White organization found
someone who did Urban Trauma training.

In all fairness, this was a POC, and the organization had hired
that person to do the training. But when my team called the White
organization and gave it our trademark statement, the organization

responded by acting offended that we would call them out (micro-aggression) and did not want to recognize that I authored the framework of Urban Trauma (White privilege). Ultimately, because I was legally protected, they changed the name of the workshop and life moved on.

As a reader, you may be thinking, "Well, this can happen to anyone." And you are right, it can. However, when you apply context to the story and consider historical racism in the mix, there is a clear pattern of these incidents happening to innovators of color since ancient Greece. In my time on this earth, I will continue to disrupt systems of oppression, one person at a time. When White women, specifically, and White people, in general, are tuned in and have done their internal work of recognizing their privilege, they can be part of the solution the way Jenn was with my trademark.

PLANNED PARENTHOOD

The racism of White women is illuminated in the story of Planned Parenthood, founded by Margaret Sanger. Reliable sources strongly suggest that Sanger advocated birth control for population control, fueled by racist ideology in the name of White superiority. She often spoke of POCs as being "unfit" garden weeds and that diverse children should not be born at all. Sanger used the guise of family planning and better health to promote population control and restrict growth in the Black community. Also known as the Negro Project, this plan was to contain all those they deemed genetically "inferior" (Green 2004). Planned Parenthood was established based on the ideas of the eugenics movement. Francis Galton created this movement to study how to manipulate reproduction within a human population to increase the occurrence of desirable heritable characteristics (whitening) to supposedly *improve* the human race. Eugenics was indoctrinated by the Nazis. Sanger went so far as to move her trial clinic into Harlem to promote birth control in order to decrease the number of births to Black and Latinx women living in poverty. Ultimately her interest in promoting contraceptives stemmed from racism, a history that lives in the DNA of Planned Parenthood that needs to be exposed and dealt with.

To do that, the leadership of Planned Parenthood Federation of America first has an obligation to publicly acknowledge and apologize to women of color for the organization's origins and history, particularly since its founder, Margaret Sanger, hurt many women of color. At the moment, there is a statement on their website that ignores that harmful past: "More than 100 years ago, Planned Parenthood was founded on a simple idea: Your body is your own. If it is not, we cannot be truly free or equal." Second, both the national and state affiliates of Planned Parenthood have an obligation to hire, promote, and maintain a diverse leadership team and board of directors. Third, Planned Parenthood needs to set aside funds to specifically support women of color with free therapy and counseling around reproductive rights, parenting, and mental health. Last, Planned Parenthood should have ongoing equity, diversity, and inclusion training and opportunities for open dialogue about racial equity.

#METOO

#MeToo's origins are a very recent example of how White women's racism pervades the feminist movement. In 2017, Alyssa Milano tweeted a viral engagement on the #MeToo movement. She then went public with these efforts without giving credit to Tarana Burke, the Black woman responsible for creating the movement several years before. Ms. Burke, the original creator, felt devasted to know that her many years of work to raise awareness for sexual violence was so easily given to a White celebrity. "We are working diligently so that the popular narrative about #MeToo shifts from what it is,"

Burke said. "We have to shift the narrative that it's a gender war, that it's anti-male, that it's men against women, that it's only for a certain type of person—**that it's for White, cisgender, heterosexual, famous women**. That has to shift. And I think that it is shifting, I really do. But that's a part of our work, too" (Rowley 2018).

The #MeToo founder talked to *The Cut* in an article published in October 2018 by Liz Rowley. The article explores how before the hashtag #MeToo became popular, between 1998 and 2015, Tarana worked with victims of sexual violence through healing circles in Philadelphia and Alabama.

When Milano found out who the true author of this movement was, she encouraged all those who supported her to follow Burke's work. Although Milano course-corrected after she was found out and called out, a better way to demonstrate her allyship would have been to (1) become a staunch advocate in support of Ms. Burke's work; (2) continue using her influence and platform to promote and uplift grassroots sexual violence organizers all over the country; (3) declare her commitment to disrupting the cycle of sexual violence perpetrated not just against women, in general, but women of color, in particular; and (4) spearhead a fundraiser to support sexual abuse survivors and organizations that work with victims of sexual assault.

WHEN WHITE WOMEN SHOW UP . . . STAND UP FOR ME

Tamika Mallory said it beautifully in her speech during the 2018 Women's March in Las Vegas, which I have split up in this section to dive deeper into it:

> *We continue to win because we continue to organize and to show up. That's what winning is about right now—continuing to show up.*

Showing up is about action. Often White women talk the talk, but when POCs need them to use their White privilege to rectify racist situations, they are nowhere to be found. Here's a personal story of mine that illustrates how White women perpetuate racism when they don't show up for women of color. A few years ago, I received a call from a staffer of a legislator who was reaching out to discuss *Urban Trauma* (2017) and wanted to explore ways in which we would be able to bring this message forward, especially given the legislator's passion about reducing gun violence.

With all movements like this one,
there's going to be division. Some people
are sent to divide. That's their job.

I placed all my feelings of mistrust aside, and I promised myself that I would give this a chance. To be honest, I was ecstatic that a politician had actually noticed my work! It was one of those moments when I talked to myself in the third person. "You see, Maysa, if you keep pushing racial justice work, if you keep moving the needle forward, people will eventually get it." The message about *Urban Trauma* is not just for our communities to identify and heal; it is also for White allies who are truly interested in making a change. The track record of this legislator showed a promising agenda, including gun violence reform, mental health parity, and conversations about community violence.

We have the power to change every policy
and make every elected official work for us.
But they cannot see division among us because
they will go and do nothing for the people.
We must stand up and be loud and be bold.

The following week, I met with the staffer, and it was a phenomenal meeting. I shared my complex concept of Urban Trauma. As I spoke, he took copious notes. He asked many open-ended and deliberate questions, all very appropriate for a White person who had never lived among POCs and had never experienced urban life outside of the university he attended. It was clear he did not understand much about historical and racial trauma, but I tried to provide a framework nonetheless.

As the meeting concluded, I gave the staffer my card and felt confident it had gone very well. Before I left, the staffer indicated that he would speak to the legislator and identify the next steps.

You say that you're with us and you're
nowhere to be found when Black people ask you
to show up in the streets and defend our lives.

Weeks later, I received a forwarded email from a colleague saying that this same legislator would be hosting a panel discussion on Urban Trauma. I said to myself, "Huh, that's strange; I wonder if I missed a call from the staffer." In reality, I did not miss a call, an email, or even an invitation. I was not asked to be part of the panel or the town hall. Here I was, the author, creator, and innovator around everything Urban Trauma and I was not even invited. Instead, I was deliberately excluded after I openly shared all the information about Urban Trauma with the staffer. History has a way of repeating itself; this was not the first time that innovation has been taken from POCs.

We are tired of showing up for you
and allowing you to stand on our backs
and do nothing to protect our lives.

I went to the meeting after a great deal of encouragement from my village. I stood strong, with dignity and my head held high. I walked in there with my supporters, feeling that this would get sorted out as soon as the staffer saw me. I was wrong. I felt like I was shrinking. When I sat down, I looked on the stage and there it was: an all-White panel and one token person of color who had no expertise in racial trauma. I was profoundly hurt. Not one of them stood up and said, "Wait, I am not the expert in urban communities; I am not the expert in Urban Trauma. Dr. Akbar is the expert. Call her." Not one.

> *Stand up for me, White woman.*
> *Come to my aid. You say you want*
> *to be my friend. I don't want to hear*
> *it from your mouth, I want to see it.*

While I sat there listening to foolishness being portrayed as fact about Urban Trauma, the sobering realization sank in: these people are not allies. In fact, they are far from being allies. After the entire fiasco was over, another White colleague who sat in the audience said, "You should have been on that panel." Here is a teachable moment for White women. Do not tell the person being oppressed what they shoulda, coulda, woulda done. Go talk to your people and make a bold statement that this type of behavior will not be tolerated. Call your arsenal of well-connected White friends and family and advocate for this injustice to be undone. Speak to the legislator; write letters; set up a petition.

> *You know who's hurting. Even though*
> *many of you may turn a blind eye,*
> *you know who is hurting in this nation.*

Well-intentioned White people often tend not to back POCs; instead, they feel intimidated by a well-educated, articulate, authentic POC. When you show up and use your allyship to empower a leader of a movement, that position has substance. It is the only way that the power distribution changes. White women, show up and use your privilege when it counts. Show up and use your privilege to support people and movements, not causes.

> *From Emmett Till all the way to today,*
> *there is a problem in your community.*
> *It is not my job to fix it for you. It is your*
> *job to get uninvited from Thanksgiving*
> *and Christmas and all the other holidays*
> *because I want you to say, "Hell no."*

Tamika offered more wise words:

> *We have to stay together. We have to march*
> *together. We have to organize together. We*
> *have to mobilize together. And we have to vote*
> *together—even when we don't like one another.*

White woman, if you are truly an ally, listen to Tamika.

STORY

Sindri Anderson and Pamela Hopkins, Diversity,
Equity, and Inclusion Professionals
White women, business partners at Enact Leadership,
leaders in diversity and inclusion

Even though we feel we are far along in our allyship journey, there are still moments when we take a pause.

For us, being allies is a way of being. Being an ally is a verb; it's about embedding this awareness and action into our day-to-day interactions. We have been called allies, and that feels really good. We are working moment by moment. We feel that as White folks, we don't get to call ourselves anything. It's not our role to give ourselves the label of being an ally.

Here's our rocky, yet fulfilling stages to allyship, in no particular order.

Inner Work: Robin DiAngelo (2018) says that if you think that good people are not racist and bad people are racist, then you're missing the whole systemic, structural underpinnings of all inequality and historical racism, especially in the United States. You're not a good person and an ally or a bad person and not an ally. This is about choices you make day in and day out, about whether you notice and choose to intervene, to stand in solidarity or not.

Humility: For this type of work, you have to adopt humility. As a White person you have to be willing to say, "In this situation, I don't know everything," even if you do know everything about other parts of life like marketing or finance.

Savior Syndrome: What we hear is that White people feel like if they "step up," they are going to be viewed as the "White savior," speaking for someone else. There's a misperception about what it means to be a White ally. White people are very hesitant. They may notice all the inequalities, inequities and injustices, but they fear stepping into this ally role because they don't want to take someone's power or their voice away from them. We went through this stage too.

Hard Work: We don't think it's hard to be a White ally. It's never "hard" to be in the dominant group. That's the way privilege works. It gives us ease. We think some people use the excuse that "it's hard" to avoid it. What some may deem hard requires inner work. It requires a commitment to challenge, interrogate, and confront your Whiteness. The process of allyship is more about feeling uncomfortable than hard. Embrace being uncomfortable.

The Unknown: Revelation should be a pathway to discovering the right behavior, not an obstacle to doing anything. White people should be asking, "How do I do it?" People are afraid of their reputations. They don't like being afraid and not knowing, spinning around an axis of inaction as they try to figure out what to do.

Courageous Conversations: As much as we can, we illuminate for people what it's like. We share that we're lesbians and often have heterosexual people ally for us. We tell them what that's like for us. If we can work that muscle, of sharing with people, "When you did that, here's how it made me feel," then we might see more and more behaviors start to change. Sometimes it's exhausting and we just move on, but there's something in that dialogue that can be really powerful. Not everyone feels skilled to have that conversation.

Getting through uncomfortable conversations is about having that Zen moment so you can step back and review your feelings.

Be Clear: In the moment-to-moment, showing up as an ally and then sometimes not can be confusing. If you have clear communication, then people know what to expect. Setting the context allows White people to verbalize, "Here's what I am aiming for." Understand that this isn't one conversation you're having. Be open to sharing with POCs: "Hey, you're going to see some of this from me. I want your feedback." There are moments when bias is going to take over. Forgive yourself if this happens. It's about "Do I have the ability to notice that?" or "Do I have people in my life to notice that?" This sets the stage for the work to become a learning opportunity. We don't want to be in the spiral of shaming.

Research done by the *New York Times* shows that racism is pervasive and exists as a routine operating procedure in the lives of POCs (Harmon 2020). It assumes that racism is everywhere, every day. But not everyone can acknowledge that. When we work in corporate spaces, there's this subtle thread of power and privilege that is rarely acknowledged. How do we find space to open those conversations so White people do not start shutting down and instead raise awareness and develop critical consciousness? As White women, we know that it is so important to keep trying to have these conversations. We ask people to sign up for the whole process: humility, sitting in discomfort, owning the stakes, impact. That's still a big obstacle. People want to still say, "Oh that was just a joke," "You know me, I didn't mean that," instead of saying, "OMG, I'm so sorry," and taking responsibility for the pain caused by their actions.

What we are seeing in group spaces right now is White people getting all emotional, crying a lot, and getting attention. It's possibly a stage. Can we help people see if their tears are really empathy? The last thing we want is for people to suppress. But the center must always be about empathy, not about the self.

The most important characteristic of being an ally is acknowledgment, of the racism, the inequities, and their pervasiveness, everywhere, every day. An ally is a person who's not in denial. Second, White people continually live in structures that reinforce White power and privilege. Start thinking about how you face that, the degrees to which you feel you can influence it. A White ally is someone who regularly goes from questioning to taking action.

PART III

THE PURSUIT OF RACIAL JUSTICE

Dear White People,

No one is asking you to apologize for your ancestors.

We are asking you to dismantle the systems of oppression they built, that you maintain and benefit from.

CHAPTER 8

STEPS TOWARD AN INCLUSIVE JOURNEY

This chapter will help you learn the definitions of alliances and relationships between oppressed groups and those with power/ privilege who want to support such groups. I also provide definitions and examples that cover the spectrum of alliance work, including (1) Intentional Alliances, (2) Poor Alliances, (3) Levels of Alliances, and (4) Alliance Models for Consideration, all pre-existing models for review.

In the next chapter, I introduce my Ally Identity Model, created specifically for allies invested in creating alliances for the pursuit of racial justice. As the reader, you may find yourself in any of these categories or connected to one model over another. There is always room for growth and improvement within and between models. Consider allyship a journey, just like anything else worthwhile in our lives.

INTENTIONAL ALLIANCES

Throughout history, alliances and coalitional cooperation have been formed by independent groups of different races for a common goal or because of a prevailing threat (Pietraszewski, Cosmides, and Tooby 2014). The common understanding of alliances, whether political, personal, or economic, is that alliances are generally formed at the meeting point of common interests, not by one party demanding that the other meet them on their own terms or not at all. For the purpose of this book, allyship is mostly described as a fixed point rather than as a negotiated point or place of agreement between two allies, as described earlier. If you identify as White and are reading this section, you may feel that forming an alliance for racial justice should not be unilaterally defined by the terms of a person of color (POC). I would challenge the reader to consider that POCs have already conformed to White norms, customs, and values; therefore, independence for a POC has never been established for the purpose of fulfilling an alliance based on the aforementioned definition. In essence, POCs have already allied themselves with White culture. Now it is up to you to consider the history, definitions, and steps offered in this book to ally yourselves with us. As a POC, I offer a different perspective in defining allyship outside of the typical White voices that take up this space.

An ally can exist from a different racial background, gender, sexual orientation, socioeconomic group, or something else. The value of creating alliances is the strong social impact on the cultivation of a new world of inclusion, equality, and embodiment of a just society. There are several ways that an alliance can be created between groups: (1) cultivating positive feelings and attitudes toward the marginalized group; (2) increasing knowledge and understanding, (3) focusing on values, (4) understanding the use of privilege, and (5) empathy (Gonzalez, Riggle, and Rostosky 2015).

So what exactly is an ally? Previous chapters explored the popular cultural definitions around defining allyship. In this section, we take a deeper dive into the textbook definition of allyship and how it can be utilized.

Merriam-Webster Dictionary (n.d.) defines an ally as one who is associated with another as a helper: a person or group that provides assistance and support in an ongoing effort, activity, or struggle. Washington and Evans (1991) describe an ally as a member of the dominant group who provides assistance to end oppression through support and advocacy. Originally, the role of an ally was popularized in the civil rights era of the 1960s with White allies in anti-racist activism, male allies in the struggle for women's rights, and straight allies in LGBTQ (lesbian, gay, bisexual, transgender, queer/questioning) rights advocacy (Brooks and Edwards 2009). In general, the role of the ally is to spread awareness among a dominant group and support the activism of members of a marginalized group.

Allies are people who recognize the unearned privilege they receive from society's patterns of injustice and take responsibility for changing these patterns. Being an ally is more than being sympathetic and feeling bad for those who experience discrimination. What we are witnessing now are allies ready for the fight until a fight actually arises, then it's none of their business because they are not willing to risk their own security. So it is more than simply believing in equality. An ally is willing to act with, and for, others in pursuit of ending oppression and creating equality. Real allies are willing to step out of their comfort zones. Those who decide to undertake the ally role must recognize and understand the power and privileges that one receives, accepts, and experiences and they use that position to act for justice.

In a world of stigma, prejudice, and oppression, an ally is necessary to end the negative attitudes and feelings toward an oppressed group of people (Gonzalez, Riggle, and Rostosky 2015). Allies are known to defend and transform into a protective role of the oppressed group. In the "Code of Ethics for Anti-Racist White Allies," authors Jlove Calderon and Tim Wise (n.d.) provide basic knowledge and techniques on how to be an ally. One important message they convey is that allies should not aspire to lead but follow and work in solidarity with individuals and communities of color. The authors recognize that it can be very easy to have the best intentions yet do more harm. Without proper understanding, methods chosen can catastrophically reinforce privilege and inequity rather than diminish them. Finally, all efforts are to be grounded in the structures of accountability led by POCs. When it comes to alliances, POCs need to know who has our backs, or who is with us. The fight, whether backward or forward, as long as it is together, assumes a complicated struggle towards liberation.

POOR ALLIANCES

Recognizing that there are forms of bad allyship is also important because I am a firm believer that you don't know what you don't know. One such example is that of **Salvation, aka Missionary Work and Self-Therapy**, where allies all too often carry romantic notions of oppressed folks they wish to "save." These are the ally "saviors" who see victims as tokens instead of people. Another is **Exploitation and Co-optation**. Those who co-opt are only there to advance self-interests; usually it's either notoriety or financial gain. As these "allies" seek to impose their agenda, they out themselves. Next is the **Self-proclaiming/Confessional Allies**. These are the people who all too often show up with an "I am here to support you!" attitude that they wear like a badge.

 Parachuters rush to the front lines seemingly from out of nowhere. They literally move from one hot or seductive agenda to the next. They are Academics and Intellectuals, and their role in the struggle can be extremely patronizing. In many cases, the academics maintain institutional power above the knowledge and skill base of the community or communities in struggle. Intellectuals are most often fixated on unlearning oppression. **Gatekeepers** seek power over, not with, others. They are known for the tactics of controlling and/or withholding information, resources, connections, support, and so on. There are **Navigators and Floaters**; the "navigating" ally is someone who is familiar or skilled in jargon and maneuvers through spaces of struggle yet doesn't have meaningful dialogue, either by avoiding racially laden debates or remaining silent, nor do they take meaningful action beyond their personal comfort zones. This exists with entire organizations too. They uphold their privilege and, by extension, the dominant power structures by not directly calling out and/or working toward dismantling said systems of power.

Resignation of control around systemic racism is a by-product of the allyship establishment. At first, the dynamic may not seem problematic; after all, why would it be an issue that those who benefit from systems of oppression would reject or distance themselves from those very same systems and behaviors? In the worst case poor allies act paralyzed, having little understanding of the true harm that they are committing by their inactivity, while claiming to be an ally.

ALLIANCE MODELS FOR CONSIDERATION

After an extensive review of the literature and print media about various alliance models, I found several options created for the purpose of leading White people through the allyship process. In this section, I recommend helpful models of allyship, and I also recommend a specific model I designed for the developmental progression of White allyship from a psychological lens for those of you who are working in or interested in joining racial and social justice work.

Five models were reviewed for applicability and adaptability in the allyship journey, depending on your work environment, what type of board you sit on, and/or the policies and laws you are trying to change; any of these models could be useful. **The models are ordered from conventional to holistic.** Nonetheless, they are all considered **foundational models**. Furthermore, each model has a brief description, outlines who the intended audience is, and describes the ethnic identification and sexual orientation of the author/creator.

Model 1: Inclusive Leader Continuum
Created by Jennifer Brown

Jennifer Brown, a White lesbian ally and diversity expert, created the Inclusive Leader Continuum, detailed in her newly released book, *How to Be an Inclusive Leader: Your Role of Creating Cultures of Belonging Where Everyone Can Thrive* (2019). This framework is grounded on the differences between knowing and doing. Jennifer's book is a great guide for those that are starting their allyship journey or work in corporate environments where diversity and inclusion are gaining traction.

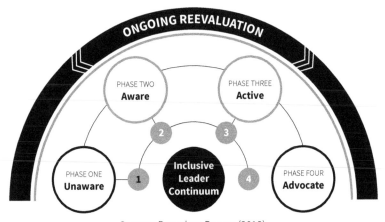

Source: Based on Brown (2019).

The model assumes that those in Phase 1 are unaware of diversity/inclusion and have no understanding of the issue. Phase 2 highlights those who are **aware** and know basic concepts but are not active on behalf of themselves or others. Phase 3 leads to an **active** ally, one who is well-informed, sharing, and seeking diversity when asked/prompted. Finally, Phase 4 is the **advocate** who is committed, routinely and proactively championing inclusion.

I am grateful to Jennifer for sharing not only her personal insights about the book with me during several of our conversations but also her willingness to be interviewed regarding her journey to allyship. During our in-depth discussion about allyship, Jennifer shared that there is energy and action in being an ally.

Jennifer said,

> It's about putting your body, words, voice, and
> presence into the situation and trying to create a
> change. By pushing beyond this model to think
> about racial justice, White people can be allies.
> Think of allies as tactical in the ways that they go
> about enacting change.
>
> An ally does not have blind energy nor is
> overly emotional; they have a strategic lens. As an
> advocate, you have to consider many factors. The
> word *ally* comes with some mixed feelings. In the
> LGBTQ community, straight allyship began in the
> workplace. There has been forward movement in
> deepening the understanding between real versus
> paper allies. Over time, there has been a maturity
> in understanding that allyship goes beyond sym-
> bols and signs. In this model, allyship comes with
> some discomfort or a possible risk to the person
> trying to be the ally.
>
> To be an ally is not to be self-named but
> something to be earned in the minds, hearts, and
> views of those who are affected, the people one is
> trying to support. You're only an ally if someone
> in the affected group calls you an ally. This is a
> journey that has no destination because the work
> is never done. One must commit to long-term sus-
> tained work, ask harder questions, confront col-
> leagues, identify hurtful language, and challenge
> jokes and comments, in all settings, personal and
> professional. As you get more comfortable with

it, you use your voice all the time. You don't wait for permission. You don't worry about the consequences.

Your job as an ally is to center voices that aren't traditionally heard, not to make your voice the center of attention. Utilize your platform, your voice, your access, whatever privilege you have; use your identity, your position. That's a huge part of the job description for an ally. Sometimes it may mean you give up your seat to someone else so that their story and voice can be heard and they can be seen and have a platform. It's a sharing of space.

Model 2: Active-Allyship
Created by Kyle Sawyer

Active-Allyship is a concept developed by Kyle Sawyer, a trans, queer, mixed-race man. Sawyer states that Active-Allyship happens in three phases: (1) Awareness, (2) Action, and (3) Integration (Sawyer 2019). Having awareness means honing in on self and systems, acknowledging and owning the truth about how your bias has impacted the system of oppression. Action is continually educating yourself and practicing what you preach. Finally, integration means challenging the status quo or using White privilege to keep the oppressive systems from functioning. An Active-Ally will witness injustice and respond to it with immediate actionable awareness. For Active-Allyship to work, a person must be constantly working on all three levels. Without awareness, our actions are often misguided. Without action, nothing changes and we take the risk of remaining the same or worse, becoming part of the oppressive group. Without integration, we are unable to grow or become aware of new ways to continue the cycle of becoming an Active-Ally and turn privilege into change.

Sawyer believes that doing this work requires honesty, grace, vulnerability, witness, and commitment. He says that Active-Allies must understand their privilege, utilizing an intersectional lens and exposing implicit biases to understand, acknowledge, and challenge those systems of privilege that directly create, support, and uphold oppression.

Model 3: Anatomy of an Ally
Created by Keith Edwards

Keith Edwards, a White male, described different types of allies having their own anatomy (Edwards 2006). He details three types of "aspiring allies." The first, **Aspiring Ally for Self-Interest**, is primarily motivated to protect people from being hurt. This person seeks to be an ally to an individual with whom one has a personal connection rather than to a group or an issue and sees oneself as a protector who intervenes on behalf of those who experience oppression, often without consulting them. Next is an **Aspiring Ally for Altruism**. This person seeks to empower members of the oppressed group. This type of ally seeks credit and some control as the person doing the empowering, rather than encouraging and supporting members of the oppressed group to empower themselves. The third is the **Ally for Social Justice**. This type of ally works with those who experience oppression in collaboration and partnership to end the system of oppression. By working toward social justice, the third group of allies is seeking not only to free the oppressed but also to be liberated and reconnected to their own humanity and authenticity through the work.

Model 4: Moving Toward an Inclusive Model of Allyship for Racial Justice
Created by Viraj Patel

In this article, Viraj Patel, an Asian American female writer, speaks about "Moving Toward an Inclusive Model of Allyship for Racial Justice" (2011). Patel states in her introduction of the model, "This paper is prompted by a single question fueled by a lifetime of wonder. If I, an Asian American, work in the interests outside of my racial group to end a system of racial oppression from which I suffer and benefit from, is that considered allyship?" (78). Within the context of working towards racial justice, allyship refers specifically to White people working to end the system that oppresses people of color. This model challenges using a binary model of allyship, which she argues continues to perpetuate the binary status quo of dominance. Patel draws on Paulo Freire's work as an alternative way to view acts of allyship that are inclusive of all people.

The following figure demonstrates that there are different states of consciousness and different levels of engagement that ultimately lead to an integrated approach to allyship. The model begins in **Adaptation**, characterized by one's inability to make choices and being subjected to the choices of others. In this stage, the person is viewed as an object whose decisions are not their own. On the other side of the spectrum is **Integration**, which demonstrates the ability to adapt by creating a critical capacity to make choices and ultimately transform into a powerful ally.

Source: Based on Patel (2011, 84).

Model 5: Framework for Aspiring White Allies and Accomplices Created by Victoria Farris

Victoria Farris, EdD, a White woman, created a Framework for Aspiring White Allies and Accomplices (Farris Consulting 2018). Farris indicated that the goal of her research was to create a framework for allyship that was authored by POCs, about the role that White people can play in dismantling systemic racism. The participants in her research study described a role for White people that includes action on the individual, group, and system levels: highlighting the importance of learning and unlearning, self-work, and a consistent commitment to this work.

According to Farris, this framework was developed using a Critical Race Theory (CRT) lens and keeps race and racism at the center. Social justice is a core tenant of CRT and should be the driver of White allies.

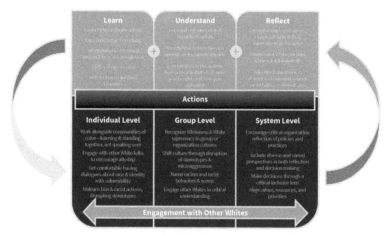

Source: Based on Farris Consulting (2018).

These models are all a great start. You will see that there are simple models and more complex academic models. Again, each one will appeal to different readers. But while compelling the reader to acknowledge structural racism, these models fall short of issuing a "call to action" that would challenge the power structures underlying racism. Instead, they primarily emphasize White people's individual responsibility to unlearn racism and convince others of White supremacy's existence.

In the next and final chapters, I introduce my Ally Identity Model for Racial Justice, created specifically to build solid alliances between communities of color and White communities. In addition, I offer practical tools and outline a call to action that you can use as a guide to implement in your organization, community, city, state, and or any place you approach of racial justice work.

STORY

**Dr. Ram Bhagat, Manager of School Culture
and Climate Strategy
Black male, partner, father, restorative justice guru,
racial justice warrior**

I can only imagine what conditions must have been like for the first enslaved Africans, who were forced to live under White domination in the colony of Virginia. To have your address, name, family rituals, freedom to relate with the environment, dignity, and spiritual universe stripped away must have been shocking, painful, and overwhelming. It's unfathomable for me to understand the depths of psychopathology and sociopathy that perpetuated more than 400 years of racial oppression against Black bodies, minds, and spirits.

The consequences of this collective trauma were massive and continue to impact people of African heritage across the United States and around the world. It is also a matter of deep respect to acknowledge the genocide committed against the Indigenous peoples of this land. The insidious nature of these cultural atrocities raises two existential questions deep within me: What is White privilege, and what is an ally?

In 1988, Peggy McIntosh (2007) wrote her famous essay on White privilege in which she described 50 different ways Black people are disadvantaged or underprivileged because of their skin color. The way McIntosh unpacked White privilege about 30 years ago was to illuminate a set of unearned benefits or circumstances inherited by White people because of their racial identity. Perhaps this was alarming news for some White people at the time, but it neglected to examine the sadistic and narcissistic aspects of racism perpetuated against Black people, hence giving beneficiaries of White privilege a distorted sense of superiority. This belief that social status acquired from systemic oppression is a privilege can be counteracted through positive allyship.

This kind of allyship, which entails the deconstruction of White privilege, is the result of White people building healthy relationships with Black people through a process of interrogating racism, systems of oppression, and Whiteness. **Positive allyship** is a process that involves so much more than a workshop, a class on cultural competency, or good intentions. It requires honesty, openness, vulnerability, and yielding of control. In other words, an ally must be willing to acknowledge their limitations, accept responsibility for their complicity, and agree to do "ally work."

It takes more than a village to heal a child. We need allies whose liberation is aligned with ours to cross the color line and engage in the process of self-healing with us. Not too long ago, a White expert on race relations from Virginia State University and myself were invited to develop a workshop to address the secondary trauma experienced by social justice activists in our community.

On the other hand, at times I have encountered a White person purporting to be an ally but they discount the impact of racism and systems of opression on Black people, the way they hold interracial spaces can trigger traumatic responses. Unfortunately, I was adversely affected by a process where the lead facilitator lacked the necessary tools to hold a liberated space for Black people. Although she had good intentions, it was imperative for her to put in the "ally work" to learn about White privilege, White fragility, White supremacy, and Black Lives Matter.

We also discussed the necessity of helping activists build up resilience to the distress caused by dealing with the trauma of witnessing brutal killings of unarmed Black men and women on social media. Furthermore, we deliberated about the critical importance of recruiting a cohort of diverse leaders from grassroots organizations to examine systemic causes of police shootings. The purpose of this workshop was to explore and interpret the root causes of racial injustice in the greater Richmond community. Through dialogue, dramatization, and drumming, participants shared experiences of the many ways systemic racism affects individuals, families, organizations, and major institutions of human interaction. Ultimately, my ally supported, endorsed, and actively promoted building resilience for challenging systemic racism.

CHAPTER 9

THE PURSUIT OF RACIAL JUSTICE

As you read in Part I, I have been asked on more than one occasion for a guide that can be used to dispel the myths, educate on proper racial justice etiquette, map out the journey, and finally support White people as they struggle through this unknown territory. Sound information about building a racial justice framework cannot come from a White worldview. The perspective I offer on the spectrum is positioned from the lens of a woman of color, a psychologist, a racial justice warrior who can guide your growth and development in this area.

Does being a true ally require that an individual place racial justice as their highest value, so high that they would need to be willing to give up the "comfort of being White" and even risk complicating their personal relationships? This can feel like a very demanding concept of allyship. It offers little accommodation to those who cannot find it in themselves to act as public spokespeople or to jeopardize interpersonal relationships in the name of social change and racial justice. I want to acknowledge that as a White reader, you may have had a visceral reaction to what you have read in the past two sections. I want to validate those feelings. I, too, have been there myself when struggling with the complexity of my own privilege.

I offer the Ally Identity Model (AIM) so that White allies can choose which stage feels most comfortable and be honest with themselves and authentic about the stage that they choose to engage in. If what you are able to do is be a supporter, then that is all that is required, with a warning to control the urge of wanting to represent oneself as something else. The goal is to feel at ease in the stage that most comfortably suits you and then be honest about where you are.

A few years ago, I was speaking to a person of color (POC) in my circle about White involvement in social justice work. That person said,

> It is very difficult to find White social justice people. White people have a good game they play. They made Martin Luther King, Jr. a martyr in death, praising him just on his holiday. They are worshipping a corpse, a dead man. But what about when he was living, and what about the ones who are living now? They have vilified the living Black leaders: Jackson, Sharpton, Farrakhan. They have vilified all Black leaders. White folks got nothing to say to Black leaders when it comes to civil rights. That work goes on day in and day out. This country was built on racism and will probably never go away. I don't see us overcoming it. Sad to say.

As you enter into the final stretch of this book, I want to warn you that this does not get any easier. When reading, you may experience sensitivity, hurt feelings, frustration, and be overwhelmed by the idea that your progress in this area is slow. Remember that White people's concept of time is different from POCs'. Reflect on the idea that you require results while we embrace relationships. Consider that your perspective anchors on individuality and ours are communal. Allyship is not a sprint; it is a marathon. Pace yourself. Take care that you do not burn out and become apathetic. Recognize your personal and ancestral trauma and the idea that by doing this work, you may experience secondary trauma.

If you are not scared to experience all those feelings and more, I encourage you to keep reading. The choice to become an ally is frankly one of the most important decisions you'll make in your lifetime. This section is particularly relevant if you are White and working with diverse urban communities. I urge you that, if you are unable to tolerate what I have to say here, you may want to rethink your career path. You may also want to examine your intentions about why you are where you are in the first place (e.g., guilt or saviorism). Social justice work requires you to partner with POCs in support of accomplishing racial equity, freedom, and liberation from oppression. I encourage you to dig deep about your intention and how your behavior aligns with those intentions.

Here are the rules of engagement: We, POCs, are beyond trying to hold space for White sensitivity, fragility, or guilt. We POCs cannot afford to be apologetic about what we want from you. This book is a clear guide for you, and you can choose whether partnering with diverse communities makes sense. I may not speak for every POC, but I am speaking for those who have, who are, and who continue to experience urban race-based trauma at the hands of laws, policies, oppression, and racist ideologies created by White people to protect White people and from which White people benefit every day.

My colleague continued:

> Unbeknownst to White people, we do not need anyone to save us from ourselves, we do not need anyone to feel sorry for us or shake his or her head at the expense of our struggle. What White people miss is that our struggle has defined us, not just now during the era of police brutality exposed, of gang and gun violence claiming our children, or of poverty and drug use in our communities being treated as a crime. They do not need to pivot their intentional destruction of our people as a well-packaged concern. Instead, they should stand up to their own people. Challenge their thinking

and try to win another White person for the cause. They should be clear about their intentions; it helps to understand what they are trying to accomplish.

Powerful. If you are going to be a racial justice warrior, you have to get accustomed to this type of raw and authentic conversation.

BUILDING ALLIANCES FOR RACIAL JUSTICE

In general, building an alliance around racial justice means that you share views around equity and inclusion, support values and actions grounded on fairness, and challenge the consideration of "othering" whether they are present or not. Agreeing to ally for racial justice is an ongoing strategic process in which one looks at their personal and social resources, evaluates the environment one has helped to create, and is agile around pivotal decisions in terms of what needs to be done.

Why create a new model? The model was created as a guide to target specific behaviors, identified by a POC, that White allies should exemplify in order to confront and challenge racial disparity, uproot racism institutionally, and dismantle systemic discriminatory practices. The model will assist racial justice allies to build sustainable relationships with POCs and with other White allies. The model is anchored on the premise that racial justice allies will recruit other White allies to join the team. Roxane Gay, author of *Bad Feminist* (2014), reported that Black people need White people who will stand up for them and take on the oppression dished out to them. This type of conviction is the act of taking on the struggle as your own, the constant, hardworking struggle alongside communities you ally with. Remember, before "identifying" yourself as a racial justice ally, one has to acknowledge and pay attention to any isms or unconscious biases one has, as well as become familiar with experiences that

POCs encounter daily. Finally, the model stands on one solid principle critical to the process of becoming a racial justice ally: *accountability.* Being a racial justice ally takes dedication and skill.

Although the process of becoming a racial justice ally may not come naturally, I am optimistic you will be able to learn the right way to ally, and the more you do it, the better you will get at it.

ALLYSHIP IDENTITY MODEL

Supporter | Ally | Advocate | Accomplice | Equity broker

Stage 1: Supporter

So here you are at ground zero. You are a supporter. When you are a supporter, the first questions are, Will you do the right thing, even when no one is watching? Do you recognize that your Whiteness has power? Are you able to be a supporter consistently, without changing your support when White pressure is present?

Supporter Identity: Supporters are those who have a desire to help diverse communities. They have a rudimentary understanding of injustice, they are curious, and they believe that the world should be a better place.

Supporter Characteristics: A supporter may consider themselves a White liberal, come from a middle- or upper-middle-class background, be well educated, and have a circle of mixed-race friends. They may live in a diverse community, go to a mixed-race church, or even send their children to public school. A supporter may attend talks led by POCs, join community conversations, see movies about slavery and other topics related to racial injustice, discover diverse cultures by traveling to different countries, or eat foods from different cultures. A supporter may feed the hungry, donate clothes to the needy, and religiously give to charity or charities.

A supporter often steers away from having discussions about race but will listen and carefully choose to participate. Supporters feel much more comfortable talking about current events or other non-racially or politically charged topics.

There is a lot of curiosity and naivete in this stage. Supporters are comfortable here, and many do not desire movement toward any other stage in this model. Supporters tend to be empaths who feel the emotional pain of others and are challenged by their own morality regarding a just world. They may feel guilt (see the discussion on White guilt and be careful not to fall into the trap) associated with social media or news exposure of police brutality, overt racism, and anti-racism demonstrations.

Supporter Derailer: Here is what a supporter may sound like when they are derailing: "It's reading!" one White woman exclaimed. "If we can get *them* reading earlier on, then this may change *their* entire community. We know what the statistics are— if they do not have the fundamentals of reading by kindergarten then they will not be reading at grade level by third grade, which means that they will not succeed in school, drop out, and there the cycle begins again." In one breath, this supporter spewed the beginning, middle, and end trajectory of a poor child of color with no insight as to her privilege or the inherent biases toward the community she is trying to save.

Because supporters unconsciously and sometimes consciously alienate their colleagues of color, there is a risk of silencing the voices of those who matter; this is why supporters are not allies. Imagine that in the room with the White woman who is going on about reading, there are professionals of color. Immediately the POCs in the room engage in an ancestral nonverbal dialogue, followed by intense staring and possible eye-rolling. This is followed by a series of additional eye movements consisting of eyes getting wide, then small; then a side-eye; and, if really offended, either a nod side to side, signaling no, or a chin up, meaning, "Here we go again," and/or "Can you believe this shit?" Just a regular day at the office where a White woman is telling us what we need to do with our kids, schools, community, fill in the blank, this time it's reading. During the last meeting, it was food insecurity. "If *they* only knew where their next meal was coming from then *they* would be better off." The POCs are thinking, "If only your people would stop creating food deserts through redlining and neighborhood profiling, then we wouldn't have to talk about food insecurity. Why don't you go talk to your fellow gentrifier, they created the problem?" The meeting before that: "No no. See, the problem is fathers. If the fathers were present and involved, then 'African American boys' would stop being so angry." The POCs are thinking, "If you would stop policing, killing, arresting, harassing, and imprisoning our men, then we could start having a real conversation about why they are not involved."

CALL TO ACTION FOR SUPPORTERS

- Meaningfully connect with a POC who is passionate about grassroots social/racial justice work and a White person whom a POC has vetted as a champion for racial justice, and begin to build your advisory board. **Befriend.**

- Inform yourself about historically oppressed groups. You do not have to learn about all of them, just choose one that you feel most connected to. Begin to read culturally competent books about the said culture you are supporting and stay updated on current acts of discrimination towards that group. **Be informed.**

- Read, learn, interact, and eat with people from that culture. **Be curious.**

Stage 2: Ally

Ally Identity: Allies have to lend their voices and their privilege to advance the inclusion and equity for POCs.

If you are committed to being a good ally, here are some tips:

Do	Don't
Listen, learn, and consider.	Occupy all the space in the room.
Ask POCs what they think about the problem and how they feel.	Identify the problem, as if you know best.
Allow for an open conversation.	Jump to solutions without honoring the process.
Be consistently aware that you are not the expert on all matters POC.	Call the same thing something different/redefine the problem.
Be patient and allow for a courageous conversation about race.	Talk down to POCs or shut them out of the conversation.

Ally Characteristics: Within the context of racial justice, an ally is the second stage of development, after supporters and before advocates, because allies build allegiances when there is something in it for them. The good allies say, "I feel sympathy for your plight. I wish you well, and when it becomes convenient, I will work on your behalf." A good ally sends thoughts and prayers for victims of racial injustice. A good ally will retweet photos of a community's protest, march with them in the streets, and hashtag the name of those murdered by police. Allyship includes listening, educating, and advocating. Allies want to lead the fight on behalf of the marginalized. Allies create a lot of action-oriented goals. Allies are tasked to build, challenge, and take action steps to make change happen. White allies lend support in the areas they care deeply about (i.e., education, poverty, food deserts, etc.). Allies do not always communicate their intentions to POCs so that they can be perceived as unclear.

To be an ally is the recognition that, in spite of having the desire for equality among the human race, despite yearly giving to charitable organizations, even if you have gone so far to adopt children of a different ethnicity, it still does not make you an ally to POCs. Allies are good, decent, well-intended White people.

Ally Derailer: Allies are often well positioned (nonprofit leaders, researchers, funders, politicians, etc.) to help those who are disadvantaged by structural racism. Here is what a White male ally may sound like: "It is about gun violence. We need stronger laws around gun control because there is so much violence in the inner city. I have all the statistics on community and gun violence. My nonprofit has been conducting research on the impact of police brutality, disproportionate minority contact, and juvenile arrests." The White nonprofit leader indicates that he has lobbied legislators for commonsense gun reform laws and has connected with other funders who will provide a million dollars to his nonprofit to lead the charge on suppressing gun violence throughout the state.

At the same time, this ally has no POCs on his team; he has no advisory group of color to help him understand the community he is trying to help and is unable to make meaningful connections with the people that his project is supposed to serve. Typically, this White ally lives outside of the nexus population. This White ally considers himself an expert in the field of gun violence and exercises his privilege when needed to get continued support or funding for his work.

In another meeting, "mentoring is the answer. *These* kids just need positive role models. Most of them are growing up with a single mom who is too busy working to understand what is happening with her child." Another meeting, another meeting, and more meetings. These people often use fancy phrases like social justice, restorative practices, diversity and inclusion, trauma-informed care, toxic masculinity, microaggression and implicit bias (my favorite), fatherhood initiatives, healthy moms, healthy kids ... I could go on and on.

Here is the fundamental problem with all these catchphrases: unless the nonprofit leaders, social justice-driven organizations, politicians, philanthropic organizations, or school leaders have acknowledged institutional racism within their organizations and are continuously calling out racism, then all those words are empty promises and merely feel-good moments for White people to reinforce their savior complex, with a sprinkle of delusion that we should all be color-blind and live in harmony.

At the ally phase, it is possible to make harmful mistakes, like calling the police on a Black man bird-watching in Central Park. This is why when allies tap deeper into their motivation, they want to do better and go to the next stage.

CALL TO ACTION FOR ALLIES

One of the most important mental, emotional, and spiritual transformations that needs to happen in this stage is acknowledgment and acceptance.

- Define and understand your privilege. Own your stolen birthright.
- Deal with your guilt and begin focusing on how you will correct learned behavior passed down to you for generations through reading anti-racism and allyship books, getting a life coach, and/or working with a racial trauma expert.
- Monitor yourself before you speak so you can align your intentions with your behaviors.
- Be humble around those who appreciate your help but do not require it and often have not asked for it in the way you want to give it.

Stage 3: Advocate

Advocate Identity: Advocates become actively involved supporting, promoting, or leading social justice events with money, time, and resources.

Advocate Characteristics: In this stage, advocates do not just attend rallies but they engage in difficult conversations about politics, tackle racially laden discussions, check themselves and others for bias, speak against racism and inequality, and express clear anti-racism sentiments in front of their Black or Brown friends. When advocates feel safe, there may be symbolic showmanship such as having a Black Lives Matter sticker on their car or their front law. Advocates participate or lead fundraiser galas and invite their wealthy White friends to donate money and support a worthy cause.

This stage can be marked with guilt, and as such, there is separatism from family and friends to feel disassociated from their ancestral legacy. There is a proclamation regarding a new generation of anti-racist Whites. Advocates figure out ways to save POCs from their forsaken destinies (be cautious about the savior complex in this stage). In this stage, advocates may have cut off openly racist people in their circle and defriended those who support racist agendas from social media.

Cultural humility sets in during this stage. Cultural humility is a concept developed as a result of the increasing awareness of diversity and the demand for a more inclusive world. According to this concept, individuals must be open to others and aspects of their cultural identity that are important to them. This is done through consistent self-evaluation and critique, a desire to fix imbalances where they exist, and by the development of relationships with other like-minded advocates (Hook et al. 2013). By holding oneself and others accountable, one is able to bring forth systemic change and advocacy. When we acknowledge that our understanding of cultural differences is often limited, we take the first step in practicing cultural humility. Practicing cultural humility is about noticing your limitations, increasing self-awareness of biases, and understanding the oppression of others. By recognizing that we are constantly growing and learning, we can become better people and better allies.

Advocate Derailer: There is a reason why you are still in transition in your racial justice work. The reason is that when you witness racism or oppression in the presence of other Whites, you do not speak up. There is a subtle hiding behind privilege and the ability to morph between communities with ease. When phrases like "these people," "those parents," and "those kids" are unintentionally spoken in the presence of an advocate to describe people in communities of color, you do not take that opportunity to call out the person or question their intentionality. There is a lack of identification with the struggle of communities of color because, whether consciously or unconsciously, you are still inherently different and hold onto your power over "them."

Entitlement can easily operate at the core of this stage. Through entitlement, the justification of familial closet racist ideologies springs up, thoughts that you are constantly fighting against. You may do things like bringing unwanted or gently used clothes or food for the poor Black and Brown kids. You may become a mentor, a teacher, or a coach in an urban community. Moreover, you may not just adopt a Black or Brown kid, but you also start every conversation with this trophy to solidify your position as an advocate. You may venture into the "'hood" to find the right hair care products or barbershop for your Black or Brown child, buy them racially appropriate dolls, and even connect them with others in your friend group who are like them. You are sensitive to the racial differences between you and your child, and you try very hard to have cultural humility. In spite all this work you do not let go of

White privilege and entitlement. You still think you know better than the marginalized.

Nonetheless this stage is uncomfortable because growth is happening, so there are times when you will feel overwhelmed; however, if you truly want to make a difference, take a deep breath and get ready to move from the passenger seat. Take the wheel. Use what resources you have available and move to the next stage of becoming an effective accomplice, without any excuses!

CALL TO ACTION FOR ADVOCATES

- Talk to your POC friends about the difference between privilege and entitlement. Begin to process the difference and understand that, at least for now, your privilege is here to stay, but you have a choice on how you decide to use it.

- Reflect on your intentions if you have POCs as friends, a partner, or child(ren). Who are you in that space? What does your Whiteness represent? Do you see them and understand their struggle?

- Continually check your White guilt, fragility, sensitivity, and saviorism. Put this on rotation so you do not forget.

Stage 4: Accomplice/Co-conspirator

Accomplice Identity: Accomplices work in solidarity with POCs to create and sustain social justice. White accomplices take risks and aren't afraid to put themselves out there to destabilize White supremacy.

Accomplice Characteristics: They are loyal to fighting back and staying in the struggle toward freedom. They follow the lead of

POCs instead of trying to strategize for them. Accomplices aggressively work toward understanding systems of power while exploring ways to break up that system, to dismantle White supremacy and social order (Powell and Kelly 2017). Their focus is to reallocate power. Accomplices share their resources and funds to benefit POCs in the fight for equality. They use their privilege to obtain platforms to have those difficult conversations about race, racism, and social justice. They take action and seek accountability with POCs.

The framework for an accomplice was originally developed by Indigenous people (Indigenous Action, a radical group that believes in anti-colonial, anti-capitalist Indigenous media marketers). According to this concept, there exists a fiercely unrelenting desire to achieve total liberation, with the land and together with other people. From this standpoint, there is a "we," and we will have to work together (Indigenous Action Media 2014). Accomplices say, "I'll make sure you're well. I'll make sure you're well because I'll be struggling and suffering with you." Accomplices/Co-Conspirators feel they are in a position to exercise a certain amount of power and that it is their duty to fight for freedom, and it is their will to win. They do not make POCs feel like they are begging or asking too much. Instead, they empower them and make way for their passion and leadership in social and racial justice.

Here is how an accomplice would handle the conversation about reading detailed by the supporter in Stage 1:

> I am a White woman who is working hard to acknowledge my privilege. While I do not have all the answers, especially when it comes to supporting communities of color, I have an expertise in reading. I have been going to the local Baptist church during children's ministry and helping the Sunday

school teacher promote reading in her class. I have also partnered with a literacy nonprofit and we will be donating 100 books per month so that kids in the congregation have access to the books. Even though I do this, I know there is more that I can do. I would like to help in a more meaningful way and have many ideas. I would like to partner with any POC in this room, since I recognize that I am going to make some mistakes along the way and maybe miss some really important things, simply because I just don't know what I am looking for. I am a literacy expert, but you all are experts in your community. I would like to learn more about the factors that get in the way of low achieving students staying on grade level for reading. I have also secured a funder who is willing to support this project and I want to work with the church to establish an after-school reading program. Time and execution are important to me. Please see me after the meeting if this is of interest to you or to a colleague who is not here.

The key factor in the preceding statement is that the accomplice is presenting the proposed solution in a nondirective manner. The accomplice does not present as the spokesperson for the community; the accomplice acknowledges their lane: expert in reading. The accomplice does not suck the air out of the room (She says, "See me after the meeting if you are interested."). The accomplice provides a solid solution with funding thereby not leaving it up to the POC to figure out how they are going to fund a project that was not even their idea to begin with. See the difference?

Accomplice Derailer: Dr. Casiano, who shares his personal story about the dearth of true allies (see page 50–55), defines White accomplices as individuals who ally with, advocate for, and create opportunities for POCs. For me to consider someone an accomplice, their personal investments in action would have to be examined. During Dr. Casiano's interview he explains that, as a Puerto Rican man, he has experienced many individuals who have attempted to be accomplices or Co-Conspirators, but when they had to make personal investments such as decline financial, career, and promotional opportunities, or when they experienced public rejection by their own majority culture, they would conform to societal pressures in order to maintain those personal gains. Being a true accomplice may require sacrificing personal advancement to seek and secure justice for POCs. An accomplice understands that they play an integral role in fighting for equal opportunities for POCs to equal the playing field. Therefore, true accomplices are needed to help with connections to public resources, jobs, leisure activities, and creating new networks. Accomplices have to demystify the fear and consistently challenge their White family, friends, and colleagues about the truest form of diversity and inclusion. For an accomplice, this requires courage and the belief that we are all created equally and must have access to basic human rights.

CALL TO ACTION FOR ACCOMPLICES

Dr. Casiano closed his interview by offering suggestions for accomplices:

- **Practice cultural competence.** This includes getting to know the history of that particular culture. By knowing and understanding the history, you will get to know the basic tenets of what makes that particular culture rich in language, customs, norms, values, religion/spirituality, and its connection to the homeland.

- **Practice daily cultural humility and sensitivity.** This includes not forcing this particular culture to drop or neglect their cultural richness in order to be included or melted into another culture (such as language, customs, foods, traditions, and religious beliefs). Celebrating the diversity that a particular culture brings is powerful and humanly beautiful. There is true strength in diversity that will benefit society as a whole.

- **Recognize and address cultural disparities.** When you see cultural injustice, stand up for that culture no matter the personal cost to you individually. Stand against unfair and illegal employment practices, unequal educational opportunities, unequal housing opportunities, discrimination of any form toward any particular culture, and the violation of basic human rights.

Being an accomplice/co-conspirator works when White people start shining the light on POCs and helping to make sure their voices are heard. They work to use their privilege to ensure that power is equally distributed to their colleagues. They understand that they must collaborate with POCs instead of imposing their will.

Stage 5: Equity Broker

This final stage captures a fully invested equity broker.

Equity Broker Identity: Openly challenges other Whites when they are being racist, xenophobic, oppressive, or exercising their privilege. An equity broker creates, constructs, and crosses bridges between POCs and White people for the resources needed in the name of racial justice.

Equity Broker Characteristics: The ultimate level in the fight for racial justice is building bridges, requiring the privileged to broker opportunities for advancement. I coined the term *equity brokers* to refer to this top level of alliance and identity. A broker, by definition, negotiates and arranges, acting as an intermediary and mediator. Equity brokers push the boundaries created by and for White America and position themselves to fight on behalf of those who have been historically oppressed to gain equity in all spaces. They give up their seat at the table, they help create a new table, and they position the POC at the head of the table. They are not insecure, afraid of losing their power, or selfish.

An equity broker does "the act of bridging, linking or mediating between groups or persons of differing cultural backgrounds for the purpose of reducing conflict or producing change" (Jezewski and Sotnik 2001). Equity brokers have knowledge about the various values, beliefs, and practices of marginalized groups and have learned to support them in navigating predominantly White spaces effectively. An equity broker must be able to identify unacknowledged barriers and create strategies to overcome them. To take the concept of an equity broker further, an effective broker can talk to other White people when they are exercising entitlement, privilege, and oppression. They have the capacity and drive to move obstacles out of the way for POCs to make strides in achieving success, freedom, and civil rights. Equity brokers will leverage their privilege for POCs to obtain access to networking and wealth. Therefore, as an equity broker, you must be committed to forging links, addressing areas of inequality, and seeking ways to leverage resources necessary to further the liberation struggle and intentionally manipulate those resources to support the racial justice movement (Powell and Kelly 2017).

At the root of all this is the idea that we are all created equal. White superiority in thought or practice cannot exist to fulfill the duty of an equity broker. Equity brokers have to be free of White guilt, saviorism, and entitlement to exercise this role.

There is a distinct difference between being a supporter and a broker. I will use the example of those who use philanthropy as a way to help poor people/communities of color. As a supporter, White people with power may choose to reallocate funds and resources to support organizations that have a mission geared toward racial justice. On the other hand, an equity broker will share knowledge and strategy with minority-owned businesses and POC-led nonprofits who have a social/racial justice mission while actively working to challenge unjust and White supremacist systems. This level of brokering seeks to disrupt the existing social order and to work in partnership with their communities toward new possibilities of change, not just, for example, to eliminate poverty but also to give people in poor communities agency to change their circumstances, even if that means taking risks that will cost them their power.

An equity broker stands on the bridge and tries to ensure safe passage for POCs from one side of the bridge to the other. For instance, equity brokers built a wall between police and Black and Brown protestors during the nationwide rallies demanding police accountability as a result of the murder of George Floyd, Breonna Taylor, and Ahmaud Arbery. Equity brokers are particularly important in this very polarized time. Equity brokers are bridge builders, bridge walkers, and bridge inhabitants. They are the brokers who are trying to ensure that the lines of communication remain open. Equity brokers are bridging two sides, neither of which feels heard, seen, or understood. Those living in the middle of the bridge must see past this and continue brokering deals. Equity brokers are carrying the message that has to be delivered to each side, speaking the right language, and staying informed. They're also ensuring that dialogue can continue without breaking down.

In full transparency, being an equity broker is really hard to do. Being an equity broker sometimes feels like you are being pulled in two opposing directions, yet you are making sure the bridge remains steady. As an equity broker, you realize that there is always a threat that the bridge will be destroyed. Equity brokers create opportunities for POCs all the while correcting the language of certain offensive behaviors on the part of White people.

Equity Broker in Action: A few years ago, I was visiting an alternative school program in southern Connecticut. The director, a White, middle-aged male who wore a Hawaiian shirt and Dockers, greeted me and one of my colleagues. We met with him to discuss the introduction of our therapeutic mentoring program in his alternative school. It was a collaborative meeting because the large majority of the students in his alternative school campus were fairly traumatized Black and Brown high school students. From community ties, I knew a number of different things related to him as a person/leader and his program; my POC colleagues had vetted him as a broker. But I always try to walk into new situations with a clean slate and judge for myself.

After about an hour and a half, we talked less about programs and more about how he, a White heterosexual male who looked like he belonged in Southern California, was running this school. He went into great detail about his past and shared that in his younger years, he fell into working alongside diverse communities. As the conversation ensued, I decided to put him in the stage of an equity broker because in his story, he mentioned that he and his wife moved to Brownsville, New York, in the 1980s when Brooklyn was nowhere near as gentrified as it is today, nor was it a hip place to live. He went on to tell us that he wanted to live in the community that he worked. With pride, he talked about his small apartment and the kids and families he both taught and learned from. He could have chosen to commute from the comforts of a Connecticut suburban apartment or house and go into Brooklyn to "just work." But he didn't see it as work; for him, it was a lifestyle. He understood that he may be rejected by folks in that community, but that slight against his ego did not overshadow his passion and commitment to the work, holding hands, and demanding racial justice. It wasn't his words that captivated me; it was his actions.

I am not highlighting this story so that White people move into the 'hood or to proclaim their alliance but so that you find your own way of being authentic when it comes to the work being done in communities of color. By doing so, you will acknowledge your ignorance and naivete as it relates to POCs and you will comfortably check your privilege, understanding fully that you are uncertain in navigating these waters. This older White man in his most authentic and vulnerable place, knowing that he was brokering for our kids every single day, is one of the best examples of a White racial justice warrior that I have witnessed.

CALL TO ACTION FOR EQUITY BROKERS

- Get strategic on how you use your privilege and understand how to use it wisely; POCs can help you with this.
- Continue to deprogram yourself from needing to "save." It is only a tool for immediate gratification to counter your guilt. Journal about your feelings about racial justice work and check your language.
- When you encounter the tough times, because there will be tough times, partner with other White equity brokers for support and try to find brokers that are

further along in the process than you, check in with a counselor trained in racial justice work, do some self-care practices such as anti-racism meditation practice and liberation yoga to center yourself.

- Understand that sometimes POCs just want to be heard or feel validated, so listen rather than problem-solve unless you have permission. Electing to be an equity broker means that you have chosen to be part of, to engage in, or to work with communities of color. POCs will hold you accountable. What do I mean by this? We will remind you to "practice what you preach." If you are a broker, then show me, especially when it matters the most, in front of your own people.

Breathe. You have learned a lot. There is plenty to digest and just a little more to go. If the only space you can occupy right now is being a supporter or an ally, that is perfectly OK as long as you acknowledge that is where you are and you do not try to pretend you are something else. Stop reading now and pick the book back up when you have developed a little more on your journey. Being a broker is so much harder than the work in other stages. Remember, like all things that are meaningful in life, becoming an equity broker is a journey.

I AM NOT BLACK
BUT I SEE YOU
I AM NOT BLACK
BUT I HEAR YOU
I AM NOT BLACK
BUT I STAND WI YOU

CHAPTER 10

EQUITY BROKER TRANSFORMATION

Brokers share capital with people for whom it is more difficult to access capital. For brokers, racial justice work means sharing the stage and making certain introductions of people. It means shouting people out on social media and sharing with them so that their work gets highlighted. It may mean suggesting certain lists of panelists that conference organizers aren't even thinking about because they're not thinking about diversity.

Reader, it's time to choose: National Football League (NFL) or Ben & Jerry's?

One of the most controversial topics of this century occurred when San Francisco 49ers' quarterback, Colin Kaepernick, who is biracial (half Black/White), decided to sit rather than stand during the playing of the U.S. national anthem. Many view the anthem as a national symbol, to show appreciation for this country's liberty and American principles such as "freedom for all." This was the beginning of his protest against racial injustice and systematic oppression. After being asked by a veteran to take a knee rather than sit, as a demonstration of protest, Kaepernick obliged. Taking a knee during the national anthem drew a lot of attention, both good and bad, for Kaepernick. His decision to use his platform to protest against police brutality, oppression, and racism led to being blackballed and to the premature ending of a promising football career. When questioned about the reasoning behind his decision to take a knee, Kaepernick stated that it was impossible for him to participate and show pride in a flag and in a country that oppresses people of color (POCs). His protest spread like wildfire and intensified when comments related to firing players who protest the anthem were made. Kneeling for injustice became synonymous with disrespecting the flag. Instead of those in positions of power taking this opportunity to reevaluate institutional racism in policing practices, to acknowledge this blatant discriminatory behavior, and to hold those culpable accountable, many White people began to spew anger, hatred, and racist rhetoric.

Eventually, Kaepernick opted out of his contract, became a free agent, and yet remains unsigned. Many Black athletes felt that the conversation would have been different if White players joined in and became part of the movement. When someone with privilege takes a stand and speaks up, it changes the conversation. Others thought that if equity brokers boycotted attending and viewing football games, the protest would not have been in vain. The statement would have been loud and the NFL would have listened.

Here's a very different public response. Ben & Jerry's made a bold statement against White supremacy following the death of George Floyd. The company has publicly voiced its alignment with the Black Lives Matter movement and the need to call out systemic racism (see "7 Ways We Know Systemic Racism Is Real" 2016). Ben & Jerry's stated that it stands with victims of murder, marginalized people, and those who are oppressed. In its statement about racism and police brutality, it provided a resounding call to all those who benefit from White privilege to use their voice against the system. The company called out the racist and prejudicial system that treats Black bodies as if they are disposable.

Additionally, Ben & Jerry's urged the dismantling of White supremacy wherever it exists with these specific steps. First, our government would need to create a process of healing and reconciliation. Next, Congress would have to pass House of Representative, Bill Number 40 (HR40, a bill that studies the effects of slavery and reparations) and recommend the appropriate remedies to slavery and discrimination followed by the creation of a national task force to end racial violence and increase police accountability. Finally, they recommended a call to the Department of Justice to reinvigorate the Civil Rights Division.

Ben & Jerry's, unlike the NFL, did not hold back when making this statement. We need more people like them.

Your turn. In today's society of covert and overt manifestations of racism, how does an equity broker challenge this system? This means fully confronting the huge gap between haves and have-nots, changing a system that fails to make possible a life of dignity for great swaths of society, untangling the immigration crisis, and solving the conundrum of urban public education.

Who will you be?

EFFECTIVELY MEETING THE CHALLENGES

How do you create balance and continue to do this work when it gets hard? Here are some situations equity brokers face as described by a focus group of White equity brokers and some suggestions for how to keep going.

WHEN YOU FEEL OVERWHELMED BY ALL THE THINGS YOU DON'T KNOW

When you're White, you have to intentionally pay attention and learn about the experiences of POCs. It is not your lived experience. There's so much to learn.

You might be met with gratitude in some quarters for wanting to be called an equity broker. But you may also be met with anger and frustration. That anger has huge historical precedent and has been building for all the right reasons and all the most tragic reasons. You might be the recipient of that, or you may be in the way of that. This is our country's history. It is built into our society. It is built into our workplaces which are a microcosm of society. The playing field is not level. White people are waking up to that. But it's something that POCs have known for generations. That anger, that impatience, is justified. It may scare you away or you may personalize it. It's important to personalize it only inasmuch as it motivates you to action. Don't personalize it to the point where you give up and retreat.

At those moments, White people may have to ask POCs for their forbearance and forgiveness as they hold some space while White folks are awkwardly leaning and trying to move forward. The important message is that you shouldn't personalize it. It is bigger than you. It's not about you. It's about the culture you grew up in. It's about our country's willful blindness to the harm that's been caused to POCs over the generations.

WHEN YOU WANT TO RETREAT BECAUSE IT FEELS UNSAFE AND IT FEELS TOO HARD

The best things in life are hard. Daily, many Americans work hard to stay in shape, to eat healthily, to succeed professionally, and to save money. Why should this be any different? White people need to work hard to show up in this society that has systematically mistreated POCs. That should be hard work. Doing all this work makes you a better leader, a better colleague, a better human. It certainly will equip you to succeed and thrive in any workplace, especially because soon, most people in the workplace are not going to look like you. Self-care is critical to maintaining balance. If you are feeling this way, connect with other White friends doing this work; make sure you are sleeping and eating right; meditate or seek spiritual guidance.

WHEN YOU DON'T KNOW WHAT TO SAY

You will make mistakes as you start to find your voice, as you use new language and put yourself into more unfamiliar situations.

For example, when you're the "only" one in a room, which you should be on a regular basis, however that's defined, you're going to make mistakes, so think ahead about how you take feedback. Find an equity partner who you can lean on. Find a POC who you can build trust with across differences. Find a co-traveler on your own journey to brokership. Are you authentic about being an equity broker in a real way? Try not to get defensive or make a superficial apology that doesn't accomplish anything. Because you are going to need to apologize. And you will need to mean it. And you will really need to understand the difference between intent versus impact.

WHEN YOU MISTAKENLY FOCUS ON "GOOD PEOPLE"

Just because we are good people does not mean that our impact is always what we intend it to be. The very definition of not understanding cultural differences is that your impact is not always going to be what you intended it to be. You can have a good heart, you can have friends of color, you can be married to a person of color, and it doesn't mean you have a handle on being an equity broker. That's a learning process. But the beginning stages can be pretty tough. You have to humble yourself. You have to be endlessly curious. You have to be resilient to tough feedback. You have to continue to invest. You have to have faith.

When you're an equity broker and you're on the front lines and you're waking up and it's recent and you're trying to do everything you can, you can get yourself into real trouble from a health perspective. You just don't have that resilience built up, and it's traumatizing to learn everything you're learning for the first time to fight the battle, to speak the truth, to call your congresspeople, to getting arrested for something you believe in. Remember to pace yourself; it's a marathon, not a sprint.

FINAL THOUGHTS

I want you to know that by committing to a daily practice of anti-racism and becoming an equity broker, you will become the best version of yourself. You will have an opportunity to break cycles of violence and oppression. You will be the one to stop the centuries of wrongdoing toward other human beings just because of the color of their skin. You will engage in vulnerability and that makes you show up more authentically in all of the spaces that you occupy. Your heart will be filled; your spirit will be lifted; you will feel lighter because you are no longer carrying the sins of your ancestors. You will have a powerful testimony filled with challenges, obstacles, setbacks, and ultimate triumph. You will help your brothers and sisters of color carry the heavy burdens, you will fight for their liberation and freedom, and you will make the nation a better place. You will be remembered as a great racial justice warrior, a change agent, a trailblazer. You will have left your mark in this world and your legacy will live on through your children and their children!

"People will forget what you said. People will forget what you did. But people will never forget how you made them feel."

—Maya Angelou

A **supporter** engages, an **ally** pushes their own comfort level, an **advocate** challenges people around them, and an **accomplice** gives voice to the voiceless. You have the opportunity to be an **equity broker**. Will you take it?

RESOURCES

ESSENTIAL VIEWING FOR RACIAL LITERACY (CO-CREATED WITH KRISTINE BROWN)

BOOKS

Akbar, Maysa. *Urban Trauma: A Legacy of Racism.* Hartford, CT: Publish Your Purpose Press, 2017.

Alexander, Michelle. *The New Jim Crow: Mass Incarceration in the Age of Colorblindness.* New York: The New Press, 2012.

Anderson, Carol. *White Rage: The Unspoken Truth of Our Racial Divide.* New York: Bloomsbury, 2017.

Angelou, Maya. *All of Her Work.*

Beecher Stowe, Harriet. *Uncle Tom's Cabin.* Mineola, NY: Dover Publications, 2005 (1852).

Bridges, Ruby, and Margo Lundell. *Through My Eyes.* New York: Scholastic, 1999.

Butler, Paul. *Chokehold: Policing Black Men.* New York: The New Press, 2017.

DiAngelo, Robin. *White Fragility: Why It's So Hard for White People to Talk about Racism.* Boston: Beacon Press, 2018.

Douglass, Frederick. *My Bondage My Freedom.* Overland Park, KS: Digireads.com Publishing, 2018 (1855).

Dyson, Michael Eric. *Debating Race with Michael Eric Dyson.* New York: Basic Books, 2007.

Dyson, Michael Eric. *Tears We Cannot Stop: A Sermon to White America.* New York: St. Martin's Press, 2017.

Eddo-Lodge, Reni. *Why I'm No Longer Talking to White People about Race.* New York: Bloomsbury, 2019.

Grier, William H., and Price M. Cobbs. *Black Rage.* Eugene, OR: Wipf and Stock Publishers, 2000.

Kendi, Ibram X. *How to Be an Anti-Racist.* London: Oneworld, 2019.

Kendi, Ibram X. *Stamped from the Beginning: The Definitive History of Racist Ideas in America*. New York: Hatchett Books, 2017.

Lowery, Wesley. *"They Can't Kill Us All": Ferguson, Baltimore, and a New Era in America's Racial Justice Movement*. New York: Hatchett Book Group, 2016.

Morrison, Toni. *The Bluest Eyes*. New York: Vintage International, 2007 (1970).

Obama, Michelle. *Becoming*. New York: Crown, 2018.

Oluo, Ijeoma. *So You Want to Talk about Race*. New York: Seal Press, 2019.

Seales, Amanda. *Small Doses: Potent Truths for Everyday Use*. New York: Abrams, 2019.

Walker, Alice. *The Color Purple*. Reprint ed. New York: Penguin Books, 2019 (1970).

West, Cornel. *Race Matters*. 25th anniversary ed. Boston: Beacon Press, 2017.

Weteroth, Elaine. *More than Enough: Claiming Space for Who You Are (No Matter What They Say)*. New York: Viking, 2019.

FILMS

Bagwell, Orlando, Sheila Curran Bernard, Callie Crossley, James A. Devinney, Madison D. Lacy, Louis Massiah, Thomas Ott, Samuel D. Pollard, Terry Kay Rockefeller, Jacqueline Shearer, et al., dirs. *Eyes on the Prize: America's Civil Rights Movement*. In *American Experience*. 14 episodes. Boston: Blackside Productions, 1987–1990.

Berry, D. Channsin, and Bill Duke, dirs. *Dark Girls: Real Women. Real Stories*. Los Angeles: Duke Media, 2011.

Burns, Ken, Sarah Burns, and David McMahon, dirs. *The Central Park Five*. New York: Sundance Selects, 2012.

Duke, Bill, dir. *Light Girls: More Stories. Different Perspective.* Los Angeles: Duke Media, 2015.

DuVernay, Ava, dir. *13th: From Slave to Criminal with One Amendment.* Los Angeles: Kandoo Films, 2016.

Furst, Jenner, dir. *Time: The Kalief Browder Story.* 6 episodes. New York: Roc Nation, 2017.

Greenfield-Sanders, Timothy, dir. *The Black List: Volume One.* Putnam Valley, NY: Perfect Day Films, 2008.

Maing, Stephen, dir. *Crime + Punishment.* Brooklyn, NY: Mud Horse Pictures, 2018.

Nelson, Stanley, dir. *Freedom Riders: Threatened. Attacked. Jailed. Could You Get on the Bus?* In *American Experience*, airdate May 16. New York: Firelight Films, 2011.

Olsson, Göran, dir. *The Black Power Mixtape 1967–1975.* New York: Louverture Films, 2011.

Peck, Raoul, dir. *I Am Not Your Negro.* Paris: Velvet Films, 2016.

Pollard, Samuel D., dir. *Slavery by Another Name.* St. Paul, MN: TPT National Productions, 2012.

Streeter, Sabin, Jamila Wignot, Phil Bertelsen, and Leslie Asako Gladsjo, dirs. *The African Americans: So Many Rivers to Cross.* Pleasantville, NY: Kunhardt McGee Productions, 2015.

ADDITIONAL THANKS

COMMUNITY REVIEWERS

Millie Grenough
Author of Oasis in the Overwhelm
Clinical Instructor in Psychiatry, Yale University School of Medicine

Dr. Jan Owens-Lane, Ph.D.
Clinical Psychologist & Management Consultant
Silver Spring, Maryland

Dr. Talee Vang, Ph.D.
Licensed Psychologist
Expert in diversity, equity, trauma, and health psychology

Melba Vasquez, Ph.D.
Former President, American Psychological Association
Independent Practice, Austin, TX

William W. Ginsberg
Chief Executive
The Community Foundation for Greater New Haven

REFERENCES

"7 Ways We Know Systemic Racism Is Real." 2016. Ben & Jerry's. https://www.benjerry.com/home/whats-new/2016/systemic-racism-is-real.

Accapadi, Mamta Motwani. 2007. "When White Women Cry: How White Women's Tears Oppress Women of Color." *College Student Affairs Journal* 26(2): 208–15.

Akbar, Maysa. 2017. *Urban Trauma: A Legacy of Racism.* Hartford, CT: Publish Your Purpose Press.

Alexander, Michelle. 2020. *The New Jim Crow: Mass Incarceration in the Age of Color-blindness.* New York: The New Press.

Anderson, Carol. 2016. *White Rage: The Unspoken Truth of Our Racial Divide.* New York: Bloomsbury.

Appleby, George, Edgar Colon, and Julia Hamilton. 2007. *Diversity, Oppression, and Social Functioning: Person-in-Environment Assessment and Intervention.* Boston: Allyn & Bacon.

Aronson, Brittany A. 2017. "The White Savior Industrial Complex: A Cultural Studies Analysis of a Teacher Educator, Savior Film, and Future Teachers. *Journal of Critical Thought and Praxis* 6(3): 36–54.

Auer, Peter. 2005. "A Postscript: Code-Switching and Social Identity." *Journal of Pragmatics* 37(3): 403–10.

Battalia Winston. 2017. *The State of Diversity in Nonprofit and Foundation Leadership.* New York: Battalia Winston.

Bain, Marc. 2018. "Ta-Nehisi Coates Gently Explains Why White People Can't Use the N-word." *Quartz,* May 23. https://qz.com/quartzy/1127824/ta-nehisi-coates-explains-why-white-hip-hop-fans-cant-use-the-n-word/.

Bell, Carl. 2004. "Racism: A Mental Illness?" *Psychiatric Services* 55(12): 1343.

Brown, Jennifer. 2019. *How to Be an Inclusive Leader: Your Role in Creating Cultures to Belong Where Everyone Can Thrive.* Oakland, CA: Berrett-Koehler.

Brooks, Anne K., and Kathleen Edwards. 2009. "Allies in the Workplace: Including LGBT in HRD. *Advances in Developing Human Resources* 11(1): 136–49.

Calderon, JLove, and Tim Wise. N.d. "Code of Ethics for Anti-Racist White Allies." http://base.alliance-respons.net/docs/2_code_of_ethicsforantiracistwhiteallies.pdf.

Caouette, Julie, and Donald Taylor. 2007. "Don't Blame Me for What My Ancestors Did: Understanding the Impact of Collective White Guilt." In *Revisiting the Great White North*, edited by Paul R. Carr and Darren E. Lund, 77–92. Boston: Brill Sense.

Cole, Teju. 2012. "The White-Savior Industrial Complex." *The Atlantic*, March 21. https://www.theatlantic.com/international/archive/2012/03/the-white-savior-industrial-complex/254843/.

Crenshaw, Kimberle. 1989. "Demarginalizing the Intersection of Race and Sex: A Black Feminist Critique of Antidiscrimination Doctrine, Feminist Theory and Antiracist Politics." *University of Chicago Legal Forum* 1989(1): 139–67.

Crosley-Corcoran, Gina. 2014. "Explaining White Privilege to a Broke White Person." *Huffington Post*, May 8. Updated December 6, 2017. https://www.huffpost.com/entry/explaining-white-privilege-to-a-broke-white-person_b_5269255.

dasmodul. 2018. "Tamika Mallory Women's March Las Vegas 2018." Filmed on January 21. YouTube video, 7:41. https://www.youtube.com/watch?v=bOvPjSoRBN8.

Derosier, M. Michele. 2020. "Nonprofit So White." *Medium*, June 1. https://medium.com/swlh/nonprofit-so-white-960a33c7fcfa.

DiAngelo, Robin. 2006. "'I'm Leaving!': White Fragility in Racial Dialogues." In *Inclusion in Urban Educational Environments: Addressing Issues of Diversity, Equity, and Social Justice*, edited by Denise E. Armstrong and Brenda J. McMahon, 213–40. Greenwich, CT: Information Age.

DiAngelo, Robin. 2015. "White Fragility: Why It's So Hard to Talk to White People about Racism." The Good Men Project, April 9. https://goodmenproject.com/featured-content/white-fragility-why-its-so-hard-to-talk-to-white-people-about-racism-twlm/.

DiAngelo, Robin. 2018. *White Fragility: Why It's So Hard to Talk to White People about Racism*. Boston: Beacon Press.

Dovidio, John, Samuel Gaertner, Gordon Hodson, and Kerry Kawakami. 2002. "Why Can't We Just Get Along? Interpersonal Biases and Interracial Distrust." *Cultural Diversity and Ethnic Minority Psychology* 8(2): 88–102.

Drug Policy Alliance. 2016. *The Drug War, Mass Incarceration and Race*. New York: Drug Policy Alliance.

Dube, Chad, Evan Heit, and Caren Rotello. 2010. "Assessing the Belief Bias Effect with ROCs: It's a Response Bias Effect." *Psychological Review* 117(3): 831–63.

Du Bois, W. E. B. 2008. *The Souls of Black Folk*. New York: Oxford University Press.

DuVernay, Ava, dir. 2019. *When They See Us*. Chicago: Harpo Productions.

Dyson, Michael Eric. 2017. *Tears We Cannot Stop: A Sermon to White America*. New York: St. Martin's Press.

Eddy, Melanie. 2012. "For 60th Year, Germany Honors Duty to Pay Holocaust Victims." *New York Times*, November 17. https://www.nytimes.com/2012/11/18/world/europe/for-60th-year-germany-honors-duty-to-pay-holocaust-victims.html.

Edwards, Keith E. 2006. "Aspiring Social Justice Ally Identity Development: A Conceptual Model." *NASPA Journal* 43(4): 39–60.

Equal Justice Initiative. 2014. "Young Black Men Are 21 Times as Likely as Their White Peers to Be Killed by Police." October 12. https://eji.org/news/study-shows-young-black-men-21-times-more-likely-to-be-killed-by-police/.

Farris Consulting. 2018. "Framework for Aspiring White Allies and Accomplices." http://victoriafarris.com/research.

Federal Bureau of Investigation. N.d. *Crime in the United States 2012: Expanded Homicide Data.* Washington, DC: U.S. Department of Justice, Federal Bureau of Investigation, Criminal Justice Information Services Division. https://ucr.fbi.gov/crime-in-the-u.s/2012/crime-in-the-u.s.-2012/offenses-known-to-law-enforcement/expanded-homicide/expandhomicidemain.

Fisher, Thomas. 2017. "Challenging the White-Savior Industrial Complex." *The Plan Journal* 1(2): 139–51.

Fortner, Sybil. 2008. *Slave Relationships and Their Manipulation of Ethnic Identity.* Memphis, TN: Rhodes College.

Francis, Stoyan. 2016. "Oppression Olympics: The Dark Side of the Rainbow." *Between the Lines*, January 28. https://pridesource.com/article/75091-2/.

Freire, Paulo. 2018. *Pedagogy of the Oppressed.* New York: Bloomsbury Publishing.

Gay, Roxane. 2014. *Bad Feminist: Essays.* New York: HarperCollins.

Gonzalez, Kirsten, Ellen Riggle, and Sharon Scales Rostosky. 2015. "Cultivating Positive Feelings and Attitudes: A Path to Prejudice Reduction and Ally Behavior." *Translational Issues in Psychological Science* 1(4): 372–81.

Green, Tanya L. 2004. *The Negro Project: Margaret Sanger's Eugenic Plan for Black Americans*. Fayetteville, NC: Life Education and Resource Network.

Greenberg, Leslie. S. 2015. *Emotion-Focused Therapy: Coaching Clients to Work through Their Feelings* (2nd ed.). Washington, DC: American Psychological Association.

Hamad, Ruby. 2019. *White Tears Brown Scars*. Melbourne: Melbourne University Publishing.

Harmon, Amy. 2020. "How Much Racism Do You Face Every Day?" *New York Times*, January 20. https://www.nytimes.com/interactive/2020/us/racism-african-americans-quiz.html.

Holder, Eric. 2012. "Attorney General Eric Holder Speaks at the NAACP Annual Convention." July 10, Houston, TX. https://www.justice.gov/opa/speech/attorney-general-eric-holder-speaks-naacp-annual-convention.

Hook, Joshua N., Don E. Davis, Jesse Owen, Everett L. Worthington, and Shawn O. Utsey. 2013. "Cultural Humility: Measuring Openness to Culturally Diverse Clients." *Journal of Counseling Psychology* 60(3): 353–66.

Howard-Hassmann, Rhonda. E. 2020. "Why Japanese-Americans Received Reparations and African-Americans Are Still Waiting." *The Conversation*, June 9. https://theconversation.com/why-japanese-americans-received-reparations-and-african-americans-are-still-waiting-119580.

Indigenous Action Media. 2014. "Accomplices Not Allies: Abolishing the Ally Industrial Complex." In *Revolutionary Solidarity: A Critical Reader for Accomplices*, 5–16. San Francisco: Bolerium Books.

Iyer, Aarti, Colin Wayne Leach, and Faye J. Crosby. 2003. "White Guilt and Racial Compensation: The Benefits and Limits of Self-focus." *Personality and Social Psychology Bulletin* 29(1): 117–29.

Jezewski, Mary Ann, and Paula Sotnik. 2001. *The Rehabilitation Service Provider as Culture Broker: Providing Culturally Competent Services to Foreign Born Persons.* Buffalo, NY: Center for International Rehabilitation Research Information and Exchange.

Jones, James M. 1997. *Prejudice and Racism.* New York: McGraw-Hill Humanities, Social Sciences and World Languages.

LaMotte, Sandee. 2020. "Teachers Who Praise See a 30% Increase in Good Behavior from Students." CNN, January 30. https://www.cnn.com/2020/01/30/health/teacher-praise-wellness/index.html.

Lee, Spike, dir. 2018. *BlacKkKlansman.* Universal City, CA: Focus Features.

Lemmons, Kasi, dir. 2019. *Harriet.* Beijing: Perfect World Pictures.

Loewen, James W. 1995. *Lies My Teacher Told Me: Everything Your American History Textbook Got Wrong.* New York, NY: Touchstone.

Kendi, Ibram X. 2019. *How to Be an Anti-Racist.* London: Oneworld.

Magnuson-Cannady, Melissa. 2005. "'My Daughter Married a Negro': Interracial Relationships in the United States as Portrayed in Popular Media, 1950–1975." *University of Wisconsin Journal of Undergraduate Research* 7(1):1–13.

Matthews, Dylan. 2014. "Six Times Victims Have Received Reparations—Including Four in the US.: *Vox,* May 23. https://www.vox.com/2014/5/23/5741352/six-times-victims-have-received-reparations-including-four-in-the-us.

Matsoukas, Melina, Kevin Bray, Prentice Penny, Stella Meghie, Debbie Allen, Cecile Emeke, Rasheena Nash, Marta Cunningham, Tina Mabry, Pete Chatmon, et al., dirs. 2016–. *Insecure.* Beverly Hills, CA: 3 Arts Entertainment.

Maya Angelou Quotes. (n.d.). BrainyQuote.com. Retrieved June 29, 2020, from BrainyQuote.com Web site: https://www. brainyquote.com/quotes/maya_angelou_392897.

McIntosh, Peggy. (1988) 2007. "White Privilege: Unpacking the Invisible Knapsack." In *Race, Class, and Gender in the United States: An Integrated Study*, 7th ed., edited by Paula S. Rothenberg, 177–82. New York: Worth Publishers.

Menakem, Resmaa. 2017. *My Grandmother's Hands: Racialized Trauma and the Pathway to Mending our Hearts and Bodies.* Las Vegas: Central Recovery Press.

Merriam-Webster. N.d. "Ally." Accessed June 16, 2020. https://www.merriam-webster.com/dictionary/ ally?src=search-dict-hed.

NAACP. N.d. "Fair Chance Hiring Fact Sheet." https://www. naacp.org/fairchancehiring/.

Nielsen. 2018. "Black Impact: Consumer Categories Where African Americans Move Markets." https://nielsen.com/us/ insights/article/2018/black-impact-consumer-categories-where-african-americans-move-markets.

Nielsen. 2019. "La Oportunidad Latinx: Cultural Currency and the Consumer Journey." August 12. https://www.nielsen.com/ us/en/insights/report/2019/la-oportunidad-latinx/.

Obama, Michelle. 2018. *Becoming.* New York: Crown.

Oliver, Melvin L., and Thomas M. Shapiro. 1995. *Black Wealth/ White Wealth: A New Perspective on Racial Inequality.* Routledge: New York.

Pager, Devah, Naomi Sugie, and Bruce Western. 2009. "Sequencing Disadvantage: Barriers to Employment Facing Young Black and White Men with Criminal Records." *The Annals of the American Academy of Political and Social Science* 623(1): 195–213.

Parker, Christopher S., Mark Q. Sawyer, and Christopher Towler. 2009. "A Black Man in the White House: The Role of Racism and Patriotism in the 2008 Presidential Election." *Du Bois Review: Social Science Research on Race* 6(1): 193–217.

Patel, Viraj S. 2011. "Moving Toward an Inclusive Model of Allyship for Racial Justice." *The Vermont Connection* 32(1): 78–88. https://scholarworks.uvm.edu/tvc/vol32/iss1/9/.

Pietraszewski, David, Leda Cosmides, and John Tooby. 2014. "The Content of Our Cooperation, Not the Color of Our Skin: An Alliance Detection System Regulates Categorization by Coalition and Race, but Not Sex." *PLOS ONE* 9(2): e88534.

Ponterotto, Joseph G., Shawn O. Utsey, and Paul B. Pedersen. 2006. *Preventing Prejudice: A Guide for Counselors, Educators, and Parents.* Multicultural Aspects of Counseling and Psychotherapy Series. Thousand Oaks, CA: Sage Publications.

Poussaint, Alvin F. 2002. "Is Extreme Racism a Mental Illness? Yes: It Can Be a Delusional Symptom of Psychotic Disorders." *Western Journal of Medicine* 176(1): 4.

Powell, Jessica S., and Amber Kelly. 2017. "Accomplices in the Academy in the Age of Black Lives Matter." *Journal of Critical Thought and Praxis* 6(2): 42–65.

Roberts, Dorothy E. 2014. "*Loving v. Virginia* as a Civil Rights Decision." *New York Law School Law Review* 59(1): 175–209.

Rodriguez, Richard. 2003. *Brown: The Last Discovery of America.* New York: Penguin.

Rollock, David, and Edmund W. Gordon. 2000. "Racism and Mental Health into the 21st Century: Perspectives and Parameters." *American Journal of Orthopsychiatry* 70(1): 5–13.

Rovner, Joshua. 2016. *Racial Disparities in Youth Commitments and Arrests.* Policy Brief. Washington, DC: The Sentencing Project.

Rowley, Liz. 2018. "The Architect of #MeToo Says the Movement Has Lost Its Way." *The Cut*, October 23. https://www.thecut.com/2018/10/tarana-burke-me-too-founder-movement-has-lost-its-way.html.

Sawyer, Kyle. 2019. "What Is the Active-Ally Model?" *Building Allies*, October 31. https://www.buildingallies.org/ blog/ the-active-ally-model/

Scher, Isaac. 2020. 'They Gonna Blame That on Us': Videos Show White Protesters Smashing Windows and Defacing Stores as Black Protesters Tell Them They're Endangering Black Lives." *Insider*, June 2. https://www.insider.com/white-protesters-deface-and-destroy-property-endangering-black-protesters-2020-6.

The Sentencing Project. 2018. "Trends in US Corrections." Fact sheet. https://www.sentencingproject.org/publications/trends-in-u-s-corrections/.

Shanks, Trina. R. 2005. "The Homestead Act: A Major Asset-Building Policy in American History." In *Inclusion in the American Dream: Assets, Poverty, and Public Policy*, edited by Michael Sherredan, 20–41. New York: Oxford University Press.

Shin, Laura. 2015. "The Racial Wealth Gap: Why a Typical White Household Has 16 Times the Wealth of a Black One." *Forbes*, March 26. https://www.forbes.com/sites/laurashin/2015/03/26/the-racial-wealth-gap-why-a-typical-white-household-has-16-times-the-wealth-of-a-black-one/#689e86731f45.

Solomon, Danyelle, Connor Maxwell, and Abril Castro. 2019. "Systemic Inequality: Displacement, Exclusion, and Segregation." Center for American Progress, August 7. https://www.americanprogress.org/issues/race/reports/2019/08/07/472617/systemic-inequality-displacement-exclusion-segregation/.

Staples, Brent. 2018. "How the Suffrage Movement Betrayed Black Women." *New York Times*, July 28. https://www.nytimes.com/2018/07/28/opinion/sunday/suffrage-movement-racism-black-women.html.

Steele, Shelby. 1990. "White Guilt." *The American Scholar* 59(4): 497–506.

Strauss, Valerie. 2019. "So You Don't Think Affirmative Action in College Admissions Is Still Necessary? This Scandal Shows It Is." *Washington Post*, March 14. https://www. washingtonpost. com/education/2019/03/14/so-you-dont-think-affirmative-action-college-admissions-is-still-necessary-this-scandal-shows-it-is/.

Sue, Derald Wing, Christina M. Capodilupo, and Aisha M. B. Holder. 2008. "Racial Microaggressions in the Life Experience of Black Americans. *Professional Psychology: Research and Practice* 39(3): 329–36.

Sullaway, Megan, and Edward Dunbar. 1996. "Clinical Manifestations of Prejudice in Psychotherapy: Toward a Strategy of Assessment and Treatment." *Clinical Psychology: Science and Practice* 3(4): 296–309.

Sullivan, Shannon. 2017. "White Priority." *Critical Philosophy of Race* 5(2): 171–82.

Swim, Janet K., and Deborah L. Miller. 1999. "White Guilt: Its Antecedents and Consequences for Attitudes toward Affirmative Action." *Personality and Social Psychology Bulletin* 25(4): 500–14.

Tatum, Beverly Daniel. 1994. "Teaching White Students About Racism: The Search for White Allies and the Restoration of Hope." *Teachers College Record* 95(4): 462–76.

Talley, Heather Laine. 2019. "White Women Doing White Supremacy in Nonprofit Culture." *WOKE@ WORK*, October 2. https://www.wokeatwork.org/post/white-women-doing-white-supremacy-in-nonprofit-culture.

Thomas, James M. 2014. "Medicalizing Racism." *Contexts* 13(4): 24–29.

University of Massachusetts Amherst, Implicit Social Cognition Lab. 2018. "Social Contexts Influence Implicitude." https://www.implicitdasgupta.com/social-contexts-influence-implicit.

Valoy, Patricia. 2014. "7 Reasons Why Gentrification Hurts Communities of Color." *Everyday Feminism*, September 12. https://everydayfeminism.com/2014/09/gentrification-communities-of-color/.

van Wormer, Katherine, Laura Kaplan, and Cindy Juby. 2014. *Confronting Oppression, Restoring Justice: From Policy Analysis to Social Action.* Alexandria, VA: Council on Social Work Education.

Villanueva, Edgar. 2018. *Decolonizing Wealth: Indigenous Wisdom to Heal Divides and Restore Balance.* Oakland, CA: Berrett-Koehler.

Washington, Jamie, and Nancy J. Evans. 1991. "Becoming an Ally." In *Beyond Tolerance: Gays, Lesbians, and Bisexuals on Campus*, edited by Nancy J. Evans and Vernon A. Wall, 195–204. Lanham, MD: Rowman & Littlefield.

Wilson, Jeremy W. 2011. "Debating Genetics as a Predictor of Criminal Offending and Sentencing." *Inquiries Journal* 3(11). http://www.inquiriesjournal.com/articles/593/debating-genetics-as-a-predictor-of-criminal-offending-and-sentencing.

DEAR READER

Dear Reader,

Thank you for making the decision to read my book *Beyond Ally*. I sincerely hope you enjoyed it! This book means a lot to me for several reasons, and I hope that it becomes one of your favorite reads as well. To give you some behind-the-scenes context, this book wasn't going to be released until later in this year, maybe not even until 2021. However, with the compounding tragic events impacting Black communities, which shook the world as we know it, I knew that, now more than ever, this book was not just wanted by those who are interested in allyship, but it was needed. This book holds all my desires and aspirations for the future, a world where all people are treated equally. My hope is that this book helped you discover that although we have made progress in our battle for racial justice, we are still far from it and that in order for everyone to be treated as equals, we need the strength of more than just allies. This work cannot be done without you, and it all begins with taking small steps, like picking up this book, and learning what can be done to fight for what's right. I love hearing back from my supportive audience and encourage you to write to me at info@urbantrauma.com and visit me on my website, www.maysaakbar.com. Through reading books like this one and making conscious decisions every day to be equity brokers for racial justice, we can create meaningful change in our world. I have one last favor to ask of you: once you are done reading this book, I'd love it if you would post your review anywhere you can whether it be on Amazon, Barnes & Noble, even your own personal blog. You, as the reader, have the incredible power to make this book commonplace on everyone's bookshelf and help spread this valuable information. The more people pick up this book, the more change we can impart on this world. If you want to continue your journey toward becoming an equity broker, here's a link to my author page, along with all my books on Amazon: amazon.com/author/maysaakbar.

ABOUT THE AUTHOR

D r. Maysa Akbar is a groundbreaking psychologist, best-selling author, and healer. Dr. Akbar is a thought leader and expert in racial trauma, allyship, diversity, equity, and inclusion. She is an engaging and dynamic speaker who is sought by corporations, philanthropies, nonprofit organizations, urban school districts, and social service agencies in their efforts to promote anti-racism and advance racial equity. She brings insight, courage, and passion to her conversations with communities of color and white communities alike.

In her first book, *Urban Trauma, A Legacy of Racism*, Dr. Akbar introduces the Urban Trauma™ framework, unpacking how people of color live in a state of crisis due to oppressive societal systems, resulting in feelings of anger, rage, and hopelessness. In her second book, *Beyond Ally: The Pursuit of Racial Justice*, with wisdom and compassion, Dr. Akbar advances her racial justice work through the creation of the Ally Identity Model, which details the stages of allyship in dismantling systemic oppression.

Dr. Akbar is a board-certified clinical psychologist and an assistant clinical professor at Yale University, School of Medicine. She is the CEO and founder of Integrated Wellness Group, a psychotherapy practice specializing in treating race-based trauma since 2008. Dr. Akbar represents the American Psychological Association at the United Nations, where she informs psychology practice within the international community. Dr. Akbar lives in New Haven, Connecticut, with her husband and two children. In her spare time, she engages in mediation and yoga practices focused on healing and liberation from race-based trauma.

Hire

MAYSAAKBAR

To Speak

Inspire your audience and curate a meaningful event with Dr. Maysa Akbar as your keynote speaker, workshop leader, and trainer.

Dr. Akbar is a dynamic and engaging speaker on various topics ranging from the social impact of racial trauma to leading businesses on the internal work needed to be diverse and inclusive. With a collaborative approach, she partners with organizations seeking to create allyship and a more equitable world.

Dr. Akbar is a talented and passionate storyteller whose unique performative style has been chronicled as:

"relatable", "humorous" and "knowledgeable"

Every event is individualized and tailored to the specific audience and purpose of the event. Effortlessly captivating her audience throughout the entire engagement, Dr. Akbar leaves people profoundly informed and highly motivated to be agents of change.

Book your next event featuring Dr. Akbar by emailing us at info@urbantrauma.com

For maximum learning please reference
Dr. Maysa Akbar's other book, Urban Trauma: A Legacy of Racism.

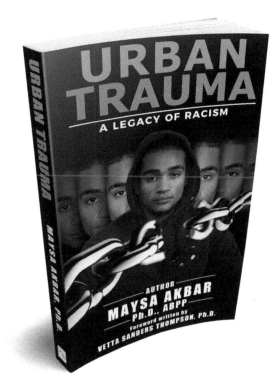

Please visit www.UrbanTrauma.com

CPSIA information can be obtained
at www.ICGtesting.com
Printed in the USA
BVHW020811050920
587969BV00034B/554